Praise for David C. M. Carter, mentoring and *Breakthrough*

"This is a brilliant book about how to be brilliant. With poignant stories and simple processes, David takes you through the key areas of your life and shows you how to break through the barriers that prevent you from being the very best you can be. I read it in one sitting, which is enough to realize I will have to use and reuse the book to reach my goals. Highly recommended."

Kevin Murray, Chairman, The Good Relations Group

"In his wonderful first book, *Breakthrough*, David brings alive for readers the experience that his clients so enjoy while working one-on-one and face-to-face with him. The tools in the workbook are well thought through, comprehensive and thorough. Completion of the exercises will bring about a breakthrough for anyone who has read the book."

Joan Shafer, former Chief Learning Officer, Merryck & Co.

"David genuinely makes it easier for you to create breakthroughs rather than make them sound easier. That's because David is a giver—he gives freely of his experiences and of himself, something that's refreshingly different. As David himself puts it—"I have packed in 150 years of life into this book, though I am only 53." It's a must-read for anyone who wants to become better—and that's everyone!"

Rajeev Suri, CEO, of Liqwid Krystal India Limited

"David knows his subject. He's remarkably good at framing things and helping you make decisions. Not taking it off you but leaving it for you to resolve. David is excellent at facilitating the process to do that. David has a remarkable ability to understand people and to help them maximize their potential and opportunities, coming at it from their perspective."

Nick Booth, Campaign Director, NSPCC Full Stop Appeal

"Someone once said that if you don't know where you're going, you're lost. With David's mentoring, you'll be able to figure out where you really want to go, how to get there and how to enjoy the journey."

John Moore, Chairman of Gorkana Group

"Half the battle to be a successful leader in an organization is to begin to know what you don't know. David is very good at helping you know what you don't know."

Simon Calver, CEO, Mothercare and former CEO, LoveFilm

"David is unconventional, creative, nonlinear. And he is a great example of what can be achieved in nontraditional ways."

Vitaly Vasiliev, CEO, Gazprom Marketing & Trading

"I think everyone, regardless of their seniority, at one stage or another in their life might need a mentor. When it comes to very important changes in their life, they would need that. David is a hardworking professional, a dedicated and passionate person. I saw the efforts and how tirelessly he works around the clock to make things happen."

Elham Hassan, Chairman, Healthcorp Bahrain

"When David leaves people, he leaves behind something special. He becomes part of their mind-set. They are continuously asking themselves, 'What would David think about this?' That's a phenomenal gift he has."

Alison Hutchinson, Chief Executive, Pennies Foundation

BREAK THROUGH

David C. M. Carter

Jeremy P. Tarcher/Penguin
A MEMBER OF PENGUIN GROUP (USA) INC.
NEW YORK

JEREMY P. TARCHER/PENGUIN
Published by the Penguin Group
Penguin Group (USA) Inc., 375 Hudson Street,
New York, New York 10014, USA

USA · Canada · UK · Ireland · Australia
New Zealand · India · South Africa · China

Penguin Books Ltd, Registered Offices:
80 Strand, London WC2R ORL, England
For more information about the Penguin Group visit penguin.com

First published in Great Britain in 2012 by Piatkus
First Tarcher/Penguin paperback edition 2013

Most Tarcher/Penguin books are available at special quantity discounts for bulk purchase
for sales promotions, premiums, fund-raising, and educational needs. Special books
or book excerpts also can be created to fit specific needs. For details, write Penguin
Group (USA) Inc. Special Markets, 375 Hudson Street, New York, NY 10014.

Library of Congress Cataloging-in-Publication Data

Carter, David C. M.
Breakthrough / David C. M. Carter.–First Tarcher / Penguin paperback edition.
p.   cm
Originally published in Great Britain in 2012 by Piatkus.
ISBN 978-0-399-16581-8
1. Self-actualization (Psychology)   2. Self-realization.   I. Title.
BF637.S4C3694   2013   2013009659
158–dc23

Printed in the United States of America
1   3   5   7   9   10   8   6   4   2

ALWAYS LEARNING   PEARSON

for

Rosie & Tom

who light up my life

Contents

FOREWORD   xi

ACKNOWLEDGMENTS   xiii

BREAKTHROUGH TO "BEST SELF"   1
Set Your Course for Life

THE BREAKTHROUGHS   23
Your Journey to Being the Best Version of Self Begins

BREAKTHROUGH #1   25
Finding Your Own Unique North Star

BREAKTHROUGH #2   35
Determine Your Destiny by the Decisions You Make

BREAKTHROUGH #3   57
To Infinity—and Beyond!

BREAKTHROUGH #4   65
Only Do What Only You Can Do

BREAKTHROUGH #5   69
Attitude Determines Altitude

BREAKTHROUGH #6   75
Always Do the Right Thing and Do It the Right Way

BREAKTHROUGH #7   89
Brand "You" . . . Your Personal Spoke

BREAKTHROUGH #8   99
Know Your Self

BREAKTHROUGH #9   111
May the Force Be With You

BREAKTHROUGH #10   117
From WillPower and WayPower . . . to WavePower

BREAKTHROUGH #11   125
Love Is a Verb

BREAKTHROUGH #12   141
The Platinum Rule . . . and Your Emotional Spoke

BREAKTHROUGH #13   157
Health Matters . . . Your Physical Spoke

BREAKTHROUGH #14   165
Gratitude Generates Greatness . . . Your Spiritual Spoke

BREAKTHROUGH #15   173
Living in The Zone . . . Your Professional Spoke

BREAKTHROUGH #16   187
Setting Your "Wheel of Life" in Motion

BREAKTHROUGH #17   199
Failure Isn't Falling Down . . . It's Staying Down

BREAKTHROUGH #18   211
The Consciousness Connection . . . Joining the Dots

BREAKTHROUGH #19   223
R. U. "M : A : D"? (Making : A : Difference)

BREAKTHROUGH #20   239
Get a Mentor—Be a Mentor

WHERE TO FROM HERE . . . ?   251
CONNECT . . . with the BREAKTHROUGH Community

Breakthrough Retreat Workbook

INTRODUCTION		255
TOOL #1	My Top Priorities	258
TOOL #2	Where Am I Now?	259
TOOL #3	Establishing Your Purpose in Life	261
TOOL #4	Beyond Fear of Failing	262
TOOL #5	My Successful Decade	263
TOOL #6	My Three "Critical Action" Items for Success	264
TOOL #7	My Values, Beliefs and Behaviors	265
TOOL #8	My Superstrengths	273
TOOL #9	Balls in Bowls	274
TOOL #10	My Daily Disciplines	276
TOOL #11	More : Start : Continue : Stop	277
TOOL #12	Balancing My Wheel of Life	279
TOOL #13	The Six Spokes	280
TOOL #14	In "The Zone"	285
TOOL #15	My Energy Givers and Energy Takers	287
TOOL #16	My Guaranteed Income	288
TOOL #17	Finding Fulfillment	289
TOOL #18	Wisdom Council	290
TOOL #19	Road-Mapping My Future	291
TOOL #20	The Stream	293
TOOL #21	My Goals Posters	294

TOOL #22	100 Things I Am Grateful For	296
TOOL #23	100 Things That Make Me Happy	297
TOOL #24	Managing My Time	298
TOOL #25	"3D" Prioritizing–Do, Delegate, Delete	299
TOOL #26	Mentor and Mentee	300
TOOL #27	Heart of the Matter	302
TOOL #28	My Move Mountains Mental Menu	303
TOOL #29	My Top Priorities Review	305
NOTES		306

Foreword

What's happening in your life at the moment? What area of your life are you dissatisfied with? Whether you are unhappy at work, want more dynamic relationships, want to make more money, or just want to look and feel healthier, this book is about to change your life. Are you ready for a breakthrough?

David Carter is a master at helping people achieve BREAKTHROUGHs in their lives. When I first met David I could not believe he hadn't written a book. I couldn't believe that you had to be one of the elite and exclusive ten people he mentors to have access to his ideas and processes.

The thing I most admire about David is how relentlessly committed he is to becoming the best version of himself. If, as he does, each and every day you challenge yourself to do anything and everything that helps you become the best version of yourself and avoid anything and everything that doesn't, you'll find it's much harder than you think. Try it!

Most people stop striving in this way for their best self fairly early in life, and when we do, the passion and purpose begins to drain slowly from our lives. It is not usually until many years later that we realize that something is wrong, that we have lost something.

What does David Carter do? He is not simply a life coach or executive coach, nor just a mentor—he is THE MENTOR.

Malcolm Gladwell talks about how it takes 10,000 hours to master something. David Carter has clocked more than 20,000 hours. He has mentored some of the world's leading business people, professional athletes, rock stars, movie stars and royalty. Now in these pages he is going to share his vast experience with you.

Who do you have in your life who helps you fulfill your dreams and face your fears? Who patiently points out your blind spots and helps you realize how they are limiting you? Who inspires you to become the best version of yourself? Who helps you develop a strategy for your life? Who has no agenda on your life except wanting you to become all you are capable of being? Sadly, most people don't have anyone like this in their life. David Carter is the best in the world at it.

As you read this book David is going to raise a number of questions, and other questions are going to emerge in your mind. Don't read through the questions. Take a moment to ponder them. These questions are the key to taking your life to the next level.

At the end of each chapter I encourage you to ask yourself these two questions:

- What will my life be like ten years from now if I apply these ideas to my life?
- What will my life be like in ten years if I ignore the wisdom in this chapter?

Are you ready for a breakthrough?

You are in good hands.

Matthew Kelly

New York Times-bestselling author of
The Dream Manager and *The Rhythm of Life*

Acknowledgments

I would like to thank all of the many people who have so generously helped me and mentored me on my life journey thus far and a few specifically who, in some shape, fashion or form, helped this book become a reality.

Somewhat tongue-in-cheek, I would first of all like to acknowledge for his "mentoring," my primary school headmaster, Frank Fletcher, who wrote in my year-end evaluation, "When David gets to his new school he will soon find out that it's not the one who knows the most who has the most to say." I listened, took note, read, studied and now some 40-plus years later have a few *more* things to say.

I would like to thank my mom and dad for being honest about it when they were not able to afford for me to go on my new senior school ski trip when I was 11 years old. This was a very valuable life lesson. It gave me the determination to be self-reliant and make my own way in the world, the understanding that I couldn't look outside of myself for what I wanted, and the realization that I had all of the resources I ever needed within me already.

I would like to thank Susan Jeffers for coining the phrase:

"Feel the Fear and Do It Anyway."

I would like to thank Oriah Mountain Dreamer for the poem, *The Invitation*, that shines a light for me on being authentic and present.

I would like to acknowledge Marianne Williamson for allowing me to share with you her amazing words in *A Return to Love*, which have so deeply guided and inspired me:

> **"Our deepest fear is not that we are inadequate. Our deepest fear is that we are powerful beyond measure. It is our light, not our darkness that most frightens us. We ask ourselves, who am I to be brilliant, gorgeous, talented, fabulous? Actually, who are you not to be? . . . Your playing small does not serve the world. There is nothing enlightened about shrinking so that other people won't feel insecure around you. We are all meant to shine, as children do . . . It's not just in some of us; it's in everyone. And as we let our own light shine, we unconsciously give other people permission to do the same. As we are liberated from our own fear, our presence automatically liberates others."**

I would like to thank my three "J"s:

Joan Shafer	– for Leadership Values Assessments
Joy Le Fevre	– for Qi and her needles
Jennifer Moalem	– for coherence, collaboration, editing and mentoring

I would like to thank Michael Barton and Simon Hampel for being my mentors and always telling me what I need to hear.

I would like to thank Jake Shepherd for helping me create the form part of Brand Me.

I would like to thank my former wife Kathryn for the gift of her love for my (our!) children and for her faith in my writing talents when she wrote in her "thank you and goodbye" letter to me, "You can write so well, and I am excited for you at what you will write in the future, whether it be as a book, more journals, letters and so on, which you and others will benefit from. Let that pen flow and your mind open, it will be brilliant." Kathryn, I hope I live up to your faith in me.

I would like to thank Matthew Kelly for being as loving and generous as anyone could ever ask for in a mentor. Without Matthew's encouragement and inspiration this book would have remained unwritten.

I would like to thank my clients for giving me the gift of our relationships.

Finally, I would like to thank you for reading this book. It took 53 years to write in ten days. Your patience is deeply appreciated!

David C. M. Carter

Breakthrough to "Best Self"

Set Your Course for Life

The purpose of life is to be and become the very best version of yourself.

BREAKTHROUGH is about achieving the best version of yourself—and the choices that this entails.

It's about daring to dream about the very best version of yourself and what the best version of yourself truly looks like, and it's about making that dream come true.

It's about finding out what you need to know and do as well as how to use that knowledge to achieve the life BREAKTHROUGHs you deserve . . . if you put your mind to it.

No matter how good your life already is, achieving any of the BREAKTHROUGHs set out in this book will make your life better. Achieving a few of them will make it a whole lot better, and working your way through all of them, well, that's a lifetime journey. I'm still on it and I invite you to join me.

Every day in almost everything we do, we face dozens of choices. We must constantly ask ourselves: "Which choice will help me become the very best version of myself that I can possibly be?" Understanding this simple truth, and committing to it, is what separates the best from the rest.

Not being the very best version of Self is dangerous. It's far too easy to waste years of our life stuck in a job or in an intimate relationship that is wrong for us. Doing so prevents us from being the best version of ourself. That's a tragedy.

I mentor, at any one time, just ten highly successful, carefully chosen clients. They include CEOs, business leaders and entrepreneurs, celebrities, philanthropists, and a small handful of other interesting, successful "movers, shakers and shapers." I work to help my clients identify, clarify and articulate their goals and to carry out their strategies. I also help them create more fulfilling, exciting and passionate personal lives. Above all, my work is guided by the aim of helping the people with whom I work to become *the very best version of themselves.*

Now I am making some of what I do with my clients available to you through this book—BREAKTHROUGH.

When you action these BREAKTHROUGHs, I guarantee that you will create for yourself a very successful, happy and meaningful life.

During the course of the past 15 years I've set about understanding myself and my own potential, I've studied and read more than 500 self-help books and I've learned a great deal at seminars and workshops in order to become a better version of myself. What I've finally realized is that the things we need to do, and to believe in, and the things about ourselves that we need to know, are not really all that complicated.

One of the visual metaphors that I enjoy sharing with my clients in my mentoring work is this—if you are in a rocket orbiting the Earth and remain on the trajectory you're on, you'll keep going round and round in circles.

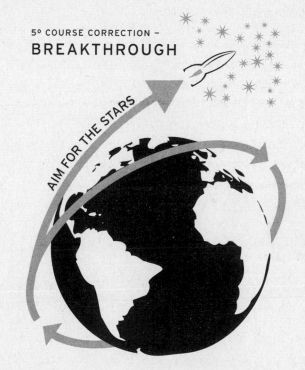

5º COURSE CORRECTION –
BREAKTHROUGH

AIM FOR THE STARS

However, with just a five-degree (5º) course correction, you can end up in the stars!

That little "adjustment" takes us to a very different place from where we were headed originally! And the resulting effect of that course correction is exponential.

Of course, a little extra power boost is required to exit that old orbit– and there are actually three different forms of "Power" required to do this, which I'll share with you en route to your "North Star" in the very first BREAKTHROUGH!

The list of areas that require five-degree course corrections, or that we may need to pay attention to and "power up" in some way in order to achieve a BREAKTHROUGH, is not long.

In my mentoring, I have developed a model that I call the WHEEL OF LIFE.

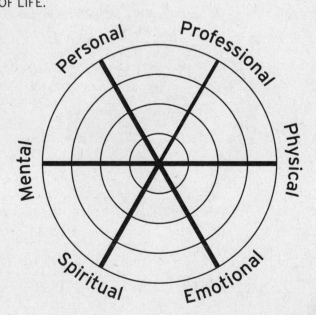

It has only six Spokes, or areas, to focus on:

- Spiritual
- Physical
- Mental
- Emotional
- Professional
- Personal

BREAKTHROUGH shows you how to tackle each of these by following a short and simple list of easy-to-do "common-sense" ideas and tools.

There are three problems to bear in mind, though.

The first is that too often we're not aware that this BREAKTHROUGH list exists and that it is such a short one. I know I wasn't.

The second is that even if we are aware of the list's theoretical existence, evaluating the key items on our own personal list can be hard for us. Fear of the unknown kicks in.

The third and biggest problem is that even when we do know what all or some of the items on our list are, we don't devote enough time and energy to putting the list into practice.

Why not? Because, basically, we're too busy (or too lazy), and until we're enlightened or inspired or motivated we don't think attending to the list is important enough.

Perhaps it's also because we don't have a mentor to guide us and to help us develop that all-important sense of accountability vital to achieving personal mastery.

We also tend to forget that even if we can't pay attention to all the items on our BREAKTHROUGH list, paying attention to some of them is better than doing nothing at all.

I love John Lennon's perspective that life is what happens to us while we're busy making other plans.

How true that is! Very likely, much of the time we're too busy even to pay ourselves the attention needed in order to have a great life.

The problem is, we spend most of our time living unconsciously. We carry on just existing, not caring in any meaningful sense whether we're fully in touch with life in the way we know, in our occasional moments of insight, that we could be.

Sadly, most people hardly ever connect with life in a "conscious" way. They drift through it aimlessly, and in too many cases remain unconscious of their full potential until it's too late.

Coupled with this unconsciousness is a sad habitual "learned helplessness," a willingness to accept repeated compromises and disappointments in life as a matter of course.

But there is no need to proceed through life as if disappointment is hard-wired into the human condition. The idea or, worse, the expectation that life will be disappointing is a very strange one indeed.

Happiness is our natural state and even when life presents us with setbacks, these allow us to show our strength of spirit. Indeed, they offer us the chance to grow and learn by seeing them as opportunities instead.

I believe that any idea that life is inherently disappointing is actually a form of laziness, a form of unconsciousness and a form of numbing ourselves to its potential joys.

And at other times, of course, we're just plain stupid. We're stupid because sometimes we delegate to others—advertisers, TV personalities, corporate celebrities and so on—the responsibility we ourselves should take for being the very best version of ourselves.

Indeed, we deviate so often from living a life that's the very best version of ourselves, and that resonates with joy and energy and purpose and happiness, that when someone comes along to tell us that life can and should be marvelous and joyful and full of purpose and consciousness, and that we spend too much time being unconscious, we often dismiss them, diminish them, persecute them—or even worse!

Such a fate is generally inflicted by those who take a perverse enjoyment in presenting the viewpoint that life is fundamentally tragic and disappointing—like today's TV and press news!

We are meant to have everything we love and desire.

Our career is meant to be exciting, and we are meant to achieve all the things we dream of accomplishing. Our relationships with family and friends are meant to be filled with joy and happiness. We are meant to have all the resources, financial and otherwise, we need to live a full, wonderful life. We are meant to be living our dreams—all of them! If we want to see the world, we are meant to travel. If we dream of building a business success story, we are meant to start that business—and be a huge success at it. If we would love to learn to sing or play golf or study Japanese, we are meant to do these things. If we would love to be a musician, a doctor, a gardener, an inventor, a performer, a parent . . . whatever it is we would love to be, we are meant to be it!

This book is about BREATHROUGHs, getting from Point A (where you are today) to Point B (your dream of being a better version of yourself and leading a better life).

This is the journey I take my clients on—and now, if you are willing—I'd like to invite you to take this same journey.

So, what is a BREAKTHROUGH?

Here's my definition.

A self-directed life change that the changer regards as significant.

Let's look further at the four crucial elements.

self-directed: Your BREAKTHROUGH is, ultimately, something arising from your own resolve, WillPower, commitment, direction and WayPower. WillPower means the power you find within yourself to find a way to make something happen that you want to happen. WayPower refers to the resources required to give effect to the WHAT; i.e., the HOW.

life change: This is the second crucial element of the definition. A BREAKTHROUGH is something you perceive as changing your life. As far as you're concerned, it's momentous.

the changer: This is of course whoever is doing the changing—in this case, YOU!

significant: It's you and you only who can define what's meaningful as a BREAKTHROUGH because you are directing it and it makes a difference to you.

Additionally, your BREAKTHROUGH will have indirect bonus benefits for you because of the impact it has on others' enhanced perceptions of you.

Win a Wimbledon Tennis Championship and, if you're sponsored by Nike, your success will be looked on most favorably by the senior management at Nike—and less so by their counterparts at Wilson.

But it's what your winning Wimbledon means to you that matters most to us right now.

You direct your BREAKTHROUGH and you define your BREAK-THROUGH.

All BREAKTHROUGHs involve dreaming a dream and then making it real.

All BREAKTHROUGHs arise from the fact that you love yourself enough to believe you deserve the chance to make the BREAKTHROUGH come true, and that you have the ability to gather and direct your energies so that it does.

Your BREAKTHROUGH is the highest and most potent expression of who you are and of your love for yourself.

Your ability to decide what BREAKTHROUGH you want to make, and then to engineer it so that it happens, is the most potent proof you can show other people, the world and–above all–yourself, that you are the architect of your own life.

Your BREAKTHROUGH, and how you make it happen, is indeed the key to understanding your life and what you think of yourself.

Of course, in our lives we may have many BREAKTHROUGHs. Some may be dreamed and made true within a few hours, maybe even within minutes. Other BREAKTHROUGHs may take months, years or even much of the rest of your life to reach fruition.

But whatever the nature of your BREAKTHROUGHs, they're yours. Only you can know just what they mean to you and why you want to make them.

When complexity and capability are matched, we tend to be IN FLOW and CONNECTED.

When complexity exceeds capability, we become stressed.

When complexity is less than capability, we are bored.

Most people spend much of their time operating at a level of complexity that's lower than their actual capability. In most cases, a BREAKTHROUGH happens when people reach a new, higher level of complexity that is matched by their true capability.

FLOW is the state we experience when we are completely engaged and attentive to the moment, such that our mind and body synchronize in the effortless achievement and enjoyment of challenging activities. FLOW happens when a high degree of skill meets a significant challenge.

Achieving a BREAKTHROUGH means you end up with more happiness and more FLOW in your life than there is for you at the moment.

A BREAKTHROUGH is a new direction and dynamic in your life that gives you the opportunity to be in the world all that you truly are.

A BREAKTHROUGH is the most exciting, dynamic, powerful, delightful life experience you will ever have.

BREAKTHROUGHs are what life is all about.

BREAKTHROUGHs are possible in every area of our lives.

I mentor, among other people, a few of the world's top business leaders. Part of that mentoring process is the journey of personal development, or, as I prefer to call it, personal mastery. That's the journey toward becoming the very best version of oneself.

Working with my CEO clients, the "model" highlighting areas where BREAKTHROUGHs may be possible in their business and their life usually looks like this:

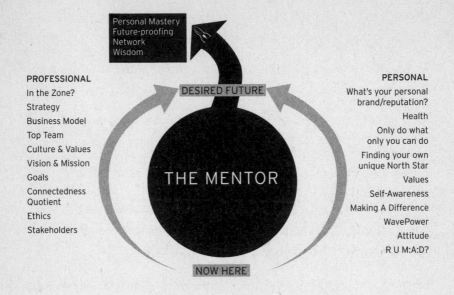

PROFESSIONAL
In the Zone?
Strategy
Business Model
Top Team
Culture & Values
Vision & Mission
Goals
Connectedness
Quotient
Ethics
Stakeholders

Personal Mastery
Future-proofing
Network
Wisdom

DESIRED FUTURE

THE MENTOR

NOW HERE

PERSONAL
What's your personal
brand/reputation?
Health
Only do what
only you can do
Finding your own
unique North Star
Values
Self-Awareness
Making A Difference
WavePower
Attitude
R U M:A:D?

As CEO of your own life, this same model can be "translated" into areas that relate to your own circumstances.

. . . .

My fundamental belief and experience is that winning happiness, fulfillment and meaning from our lives—the elements we all desire and seek—depends absolutely on achieving BREAKTHROUGHs.

Yet BREAKTHROUGHs can only happen when we can correctly identify those habits, blocks, barriers and hurdles, which—until we face them and find the means to overcome them—prevent us from taking our lives in the vital new directions we wish to go, both professionally and personally.

Our six primary needs are:

- the need to be heard
- the need to be understood
- the need to find meaning
- the need to love
- the need to be loved
- the need to make a difference

These are the "engines" that power those vital BREAKTHROUGHs in our spiritual, physical, mental, emotional, professional and personal lives—and will be expanded upon in later chapters.

Each chapter highlights one of 20 significant and achievable BREAKTHROUGHs, including:

EXAMPLES of each BREAKTHROUGH idea

BENEFITS of each BREAKTHROUGH idea

And, most important, the

"HOW TO" of each BREAKTHROUGH idea

In BREAKTHROUGH #19 we will also look at the deep emotional currents that inspire such changes.

I call these deep emotional currents the four "L"s. They are also our four primary life stages:

- Learning
- Loving
- Living
- Leaving a legacy

Above all, however, you need to choose to create a BREAKTHROUGH. You need to choose to reach a higher level of achievement in your life.

I believe that no one is truly happy operating at a lower level of achievement than the highest level at which they are capable of operating.

Getting used to a life where we are operating below capability is a far cry from actually wanting to live that way.

People who say they are "fine" with the way they are, are deluding themselves. They've just become used to, or settled for, a less than optimal life–they are in some kind of dysfunctional, nonsatisfying comfort zone. That's all.

. . . .

Central to every aspect of my life, including my work, and in particular to all my thinking and practice as a mentor, is the belief that we all naturally want to be the best version of ourselves.

By this I mean the version of ourselves that is best in terms of being closest to who we really are in all aspects of our life: our work, our friendships, our intimate relationships, our family life, our appreciation and enjoyment of the world . . . everything.

This goal of becoming the best version of ourselves is a goal that is profoundly satisfying and worthwhile—indeed, the most important goal of our life.

It also provides a standard against which we can assess whether a life situation we are already in, or a life opportunity that's presented to us or which we win for ourselves, is right for us.

When you'd like a BREAKTHROUGH in one or more areas of your life, you instinctively know that you're not being the best version of yourself.

Our work and our personal relationships should help us to become that vitally important best version of ourselves. But what if they aren't doing that?

When something isn't going well with our work or personal relationships, it's easy to blame that work or those relationships for preventing us from becoming the best version of ourselves, rather than looking into or at ourselves for the source of the failing.

Experience teaches us to be sure of this one thing, if nothing else.

If you keep doing what you've always done, you'll keep getting what you've always gotten.

In other words, if you don't make significant changes to crucial factors such as your own self-belief, your way of seeing the world and other people and how you behave—how can you expect your life to change?

Indeed, it's often been said that one possible definition of insanity is doing the same thing over and over again, while expecting a different result.

Most people want a different outcome, but don't do anything different to get it.

How can that be logical? It's true to say . . .

If you want a different outcome, do something differently.

However, as Einstein observed, we can't solve a problem with the same level of thinking that created the problem in the first place. We need a higher level of thinking to access a solution to a problem. So . . .

If you want a BREAKTHROUGH, it requires doing the "right" something—and doing it better.

So are you ready for a different outcome? RIGHT NOW is a good time to change that old way of thinking and being.

. . . .

My BREAKTHROUGH formula is simple:

Better Belief + Better Behavior = **BREAKTHROUGH**

If you decide that you want to lose weight—eat fewer calories than you burn off.

If you decide you want a new job—then give attention to your résumé and start applying for work you think you might enjoy.

If you dream of winning Wimbledon—go into training. And buy a racquet!

So, what are you going to do differently—starting now?

BREAKTHROUGH is designed to give you the information—and the inspiration—to make the changes you need to make, in order to bring about the outcomes you seek.

In practice, everybody has their own definition of success and happiness and being the best version of themselves.

Wealth and success are not the keys to health and happiness. Health and happiness are the keys to success. Wealth is gratitude.

Even people who have enjoyed prodigious success due to a combination of the vital three factors of talent, hard work and good fortune, invariably have some aspect of their personality that they feel could be improved upon.

Most people will give a different answer when asked what they want to improve about their lives. For instance, a brain surgeon might say, "If I could invent a cure for brain tumors, I would be ecstatically happy," but he might also say, "I would love to shoot 70 around a par 72 golf course." Or he might say, "I want to save my marriage," or, "I want to lose 20 pounds and get healthy again." Or all of these!

Imagine a schoolteacher who is a single parent and who, after a long hard day at work, comes home and has to care for his or her family—that means cooking a meal and helping the children with their homework, getting them bathed and into bed, reading a bedtime story, and more, all before putting in another two hours of preparation and grading tests. Most nights, they'd be lucky to get to bed by midnight, feeling absolutely exhausted. A BREAKTHROUGH for this person might be finding two hours a week to go to the gym, or having a night off to go on a date. For them, that could mean the difference between feeling happy or unhappy in life.

So, a BREAKTHROUGH is a very personal thing. To one person it means finding a cure for cancer and to another it's finding two hours a week to attend a yoga or gym class.

What can you expect a BREAKTHROUGH to feel like?

A BREAKTHROUGH will make you feel *pleased*, as if you're *making progress*, as if you're *shining. In FLOW. In The Zone.*

We attract into our life whatever we give our attention, energy and focus to, whether positive or negative.

Everything that comes into your life, you attract into your life. And it's attracted by virtue of the images you're holding in your mind. It's what you're thinking and feeling. Whatever is going on within you, you are attracting to you.

If you feel poor and spend much of your time craving money, all you will attract is more craving for money, as craving attracts craving. Neediness attracts neediness. Desperation attracts desperation.

But the opposite is true, too. Generosity of spirit attracts generosity of spirit, warmheartedness attracts warmheartedness, and love attracts love.

So let's focus on being the best version of ourselves, and attracting what we want and dream of. But first, let's see whether that focus might need some refining?

If, as the 1980s' aphorism suggests, **"He who dies with the most toys wins,"** you may already feel like you're "winning" in the game of life. If so, congratulations!

I suspect, however, that if you are still reading this book, then, like many people on the planet these days, you feel something is missing from your life. You're not even sure what has caused this. Whatever it is, it's burrowed a hole into your whole, and you can't fill that empty space.

Whatever "it" is, it's illusive. You've consulted psychics, mystics, gurus and holy men. You've sought it on TV and in shopping malls, on eBay and Amazon. All for nothing. Deep down, you're perhaps wondering whether you truly have won the game of life, or whether you ever will.

From the moment we become conscious of the world we live in, we are bombarded with offers, all of which promise, "This will make you happy." But the happiness delivered by these goods and services—once purchased—is fleeting and illusory.

Whatever "it" is, it's not for sale, nor can it be bestowed on you by others.

Whatever "it" is, it exists inside you. But perhaps you've never really conducted a thorough search for it inside yourself. If so, you're not alone.

Most of us are hesitant, if not afraid, to conduct a thorough audit of our souls. Probing the psychological and spiritual levels of Self can be a perilous endeavor, primarily because it requires complete honesty. It is so much easier to be the person others want us to be than to discover and become who we really are. But, honestly, is there any point—or satisfaction—in living your own life as an imposter?

Since the moment humans were created, philosophers have pondered the meaning of life. If you have the time, the temperament—and the intestinal fortitude—you can perhaps seek illumination around that enduring puzzle and achieve enlightenment on your own.

However, if you want to maintain or grow your empire, change the world, make a difference, reach your highest potential, with all the expenditure of time and energy that such an undertaking entails, you're going to need some help in becoming the best version of yourself.

Because your professional life and your quest for happiness and fulfillment are equally important—and interconnected—the person you're looking for to guide you should be experienced in matters of both commerce and personal development. That person should understand the world of business, whatever your field may be, as well as be capable of guiding you on the journey within to discover the missing "ingredients."

Throughout history, people have sought out a mentor to grow and develop a particular skill. Today, the need for mentoring is greater than ever. BREAKTHROUGH provides a vehicle to allow me to "make a difference" in your life, whether or not we can meet and work together in person.

What follows is my choice, "best of the best" BREAKTHROUGHs. Any one of these 20 BREAKTHROUGH topics could be a self-help book in its own right—and, in fact, many of them have already been written (perhaps, like me, you've read a few hundred of them?). Hence, rather than focus on theory, the ideas presented here are practical and tactical. I have tried and tested each one of them for myself. I have used and tested them with clients over many years. They all work.

If you make any one of these 20 BREAKTHROUGHs, you will be happier. Make a few of them and you'll be a whole lot happier! There is nothing complicated about the process. It's all common sense.

It's not a long list or a heavy read. It's speed-dating your DESTINY. It's un-common sense, made simple.

After the 20 BREAKTHROUGHs, you'll find the BREAKTHROUGH RETREAT WORKBOOK.

Working through this on your own—or even better, with someone else—will enable you to consolidate and embed any, or all, of the personal mastery topics introduced in the following chapters.

You can also download a PDF version of the BREAKTHROUGH RETREAT WORKBOOK at **www.davidcmcarter.com** to use for yourself—and share with others.

With each BREAKTHROUGH you achieve, you become a better version of yourself. And as that happens for you, I also achieve what I set out to achieve as part of my life's purpose—being THE MENTOR.

I only wish someone had given me this book when I was 20!

Anyway, enough theory—and philosophizing—it's time for some BREAKTHROUGHs!

The Breakthroughs

Your Journey to Being the Best Version of Self Begins

If you take away anything from the following BREAKTHROUGHs, my intention is that you understand how a simple, yet discerning and conscious five-degree (5°) course correction, in even just one specific area of your life (be it health, wealth, career or relationships), can result in reaching an infinitely better place in that area—and simultaneously impact other areas of your life—to raise your level of happiness exponentially.

Rather than look for magical frameworks, rules, points, or processes that can "fix" a problem, these BREAKTHROUGHs are designed to be EXPERIENCED at a soul and energetic level, as well as at a practical level—because unless change happens inside you first, whatever happens on the outside doesn't endure.

Although these chapters can, of course, be read in sequence—followed by methodically working through the BREAKTHROUGH RETREAT WORKBOOK—you can equally "dip" in anywhere that resonates with you.

Rather like a magician offering you a pack of cards and saying, "pick a card, any card," I suggest that you fan through the book and "pick a BREAKTHROUGH, any BREAKTHROUGH." And trust that the one you are energetically drawn to is the one that resonates with the greatest need in you ... especially if the book keeps opening at that same chapter!

Regardless of how you choose to continue, I hope you'll discover that you're already doing at least some of what's suggested (and find added value in ideas or stories that reinforce what you're already doing). Or, that certain parts will serve to REMIND you that you are not doing what you know you could, or should, be doing (or doing better). Beyond that, my intention is that some of the following BREAKTHROUGHs open you up to NEW POSSIBILITIES.

All 20 BREAKTHROUGHs have relevance for everyone at some point in their lives, so there is no "correct" sequence or order. They'll flow differently for everyone.

Any BREAKTHROUGH is better than no BREAKTHROUGH—and more BREAKTHROUGHs are better than less.

However, before you take the plunge and open to a BREAKTHROUGH, I suggest you take a moment to PAUSE—focus within—and ASK yourself ...

"Where in my life am I in NEED of—and indeed, READY for—a BREAKTHROUGH?"

Holding that thought, simply dive in anywhere—and keep going—until you reach the place where you know you are being the very BEST version of your SELF. Enjoy!

Breakthrough #1

Finding Your Own Unique North Star

Without purpose or meaning, our lives do not make any real sense.

"But," I hear you say, "isn't the true meaning of life the meaning we choose to give to it?"

Well, that's true. And at age 50 I reallzed I wasn't where I wanted to be, or on a path to get me there. I had the sense that I had been sleepwalking for decades. In her book, *Finding Your Own North Star*, renowned life coach Martha Beck wrote about the need to find your purpose, or your North Star, as she calls it. I had seen my North Star in the sky, but for some reason(s), I hadn't been following it. I got distracted. Bills to pay, kids to raise, a divorce here and there, a business to build, a dog to walk and so on.

Annoyingly, knowing where your North Star is, and even understanding that you have a built-in compass that can guide you there, are necessary, but insufficient to actually achieve the life you are meant to lead—if being the very best version of yourself has anything to do with it.

We need the **WillPower** and the **WayPower**. The WHAT and the HOW.

In addition, we need one more kind of power, one that Jennifer, my business partner, and I refer to as **WavePower**. It means energetic alignment, or in scientific terms, "coherence." WavePower is the "rocket fuel" that takes WillPower and WayPower beyond the resistance of gravity. More on this in BREAKTHROUGH #10.

You are designed with the ability to find and resonate with the life you are meant to be living. I can't do it for you. Neither can anyone else.

· · · · · · · · · · · · · · · · · · · ·

Do we actually need *la verace via*—or a true path? Isn't Paradise, Nirvana, Heaven or Enlightenment merely a mental condition resulting from overdoses of serotonin in the brain? Isn't the list of what we seek really the short and simple—truth, love, joy?

Near the start of the movie, *Gladiator*, when Marcus Aurelius speaks to his general, Maximus, in his dying moments, he's desperately searching for meaning and purpose in his life.

He questions how the world will speak his name in years to come, and whether he'll be known as a philosopher, a warrior, a tyrant—or the emperor who gave Rome back her true self.

Not all searches for meaning yield such a moving, profound or poetic conclusion. However, this is, ultimately, the kind of meaning we must all aspire to find in our lives.

In fact, it is the duty of each individual to find the meaning of his or her own life.

To some, the revelation comes early on in life, such as what happened to Mother Teresa and Jack Nicklaus, for instance. For others it comes much later. Sadly, for most it never comes at all. Don't be one of them!

I have believed for many years that the core purpose of my own life (and indeed yours and everyone else's) is to be and become the very best version of myself.

Although I have always found this a useful internal barometer (because I always innately knew if I was or wasn't being the best version of myself), I felt for many, many years that I lacked the compass to direct me toward the true meaning of my life.

I spent 14 years building what eventually became the world's foremost business-leader mentoring company. But as a business itself, it was not a huge success for any of its shareholders. In fact, after years of giving it my best shot, but failing to achieve what others laid down as their yardsticks for success, I chose (in a quarter-hour conversation over supper with one of my own mentors) to accept that I had failed my critics. Seven days later I handed over the keys and moved on.

Somewhat surprisingly, given that it was a worldwide business with my name above the door, I walked away and never looked around or back.

For several years I had actually felt restricted. Held back. Hemmed in. I wasn't playing to my strengths and I wasn't doing what "only I could do" (see BREAKTHROUGH #4). I wasn't being the very best version of myself. And I wasn't headed in the direction I needed to go in to give my life the purpose and meaning I knew was inside me.

For years and years I had known that I was very good at two things: mentoring and selling mentoring. I loved doing both, but loathed many other aspects of my job. I wasn't particularly good at some of them and I certainly didn't enjoy them. But the real issue was that I was out of alignment with my own personal North Star.

For years and years I had been excellent at making my clients extremely wealthy and extremely successful. I had made more than 50 people multimillionaires. But so what?

My North Star was calling me to Make : A : Difference. And the truth is, although I did make a difference to the lives of those clients, and all of their stakeholders (family, colleagues, shareholders, etc.), I kept thinking that I was underutilizing my mentoring talents and their leadership skills and resources, as collectively we hadn't really made a dent in the world. Sure, we'd made a load of money (well, they had at least!), but not in a way that truly made a difference.

During my 34 years working since leaving high school, I had:

- Two earlier failed marriages (one of 18 years and one lasting 18 months)
- Spent 16 years bringing up my two adorable children pretty much on my own

- Devoted 14 years to building my third career (after two completely different ten-year careers, firstly in international banking/venture capital, and then, in the leisure industry, running two golf and country club businesses, one of which I sold and the other I floated on the Alternative Investment Market)

- Sold the mentoring company I founded (but made no money out of it—in truth, I lost a small fortune!)

- Moved to and from America in a six-month period

- Accepted that my third, three-year-young marriage was finally over after at least a year spent giving it my absolute best shot at resuscitation

- AND to cap it all off, had to give away my beloved Border Collie, Bella

I was, understandably, exhausted (understatement of the year!).

Strangely, I knew exactly what I wanted to do next. When you visit my website at **www.davidcmcarter.com**, what you will find there is exactly what I dreamed of doing for the two years or so before I eventually walked out of the business.

I didn't have much money. I didn't have a lot of time. I was exhausted. But I had a dream. I had my North Star.

I had known for years that my life's purpose was to use the trials and tribulations I had experienced . . . the highs and lows, the successes and failures, the business and personal ups and downs; to use my selling skills, my mentoring talents, my observational skills and mental, emotional and spiritual capabilities, as well as my voracious appetite for learning . . . and use them all in the service of leaders and people in power who have the WillPower, WayPower and WavePower to Make : A : Difference. And now was my chance!

I am a keen reader of personal development books. I have an intuitive sense of what to buy and read. I am energetically drawn to books and authors. And sometimes, as in the case of my dear friend Peter Leach, who gave me Matthew Kelly's book *The Seven Levels of Intimacy* to read when I was going through the end of my third marriage, I read books that are given to me by friends whose opinion I trust.

One day though, and I still have no idea how it happened, I "found" a book in my travel bag while on a trip to Nigeria to visit a potential new client. The book was Malcolm Gladwell's *Outliers*. (By the way, if you're reading this and thinking, *"Now* I know why David, uncharacteristically, never said thank you for that book" . . . this would be a good time to own up!)

I was hooked when I opened the book at random somewhere near the beginning and started reading all about one of the biggest influences on my life—The Beatles. The author was making the case that The Beatles (and Bill Gates and Larry Ellison and other noteworthy examples of excellence) had not been lucky or talented alone, but had all devoted more than 10,000 hours to perfecting their craft to gain their competitive cutting edge.

I worked out that to date I had spent some 19,000 hours during the previous 14 years as a mentor to CEOs. And guess what? I had walked away from my old firm with a portfolio of skills and a depth of knowledge unrivalled by others in my chosen field.

I had a network to die for. And it's even better now!

I had developed a toolkit of exercises and diagnostics that were proven and reliable ways to give clients exponential advances in short timeframes.

One of my frustrations, sadly, was that too many of my former colleagues felt my newly discovered interventions were more akin to "voodoo" than to the "serious business" of business mentoring!

Over the previous 14 years I had devoted at least 25 percent of my time to learning how to get better at my craft—14 years of trying things out, rejecting most of them, adapting a few, and then really fine-tuning my skills and practicing those I knew worked.

Walked away with nothing? Gosh! I had walked away with EVERYTHING.

Everything I needed was already inside me. Just as you'll discover everything you need is already inside you.

At that point I knew where the compass was pointing. Toward my own personal unique North Star: mentoring only leaders and people in a position of power and influence, who can make a difference—to help them actually make that difference—and to raise the consciousness and capability of their organizations by raising their own personal consciousness and capability.

I now had both my life's purpose and my meaning.

I was completely aligned with my North Star.

So, what's your North Star? . . .

Jack Nicholson had already been an actor for many years, when on accepting his Oscar for *One Flew Over the Cuckoo's Nest,* he uttered one of my favorite ever quotes on this subject:

"Twenty years of hard work and training to become an overnight sensation."

I don't accept that it's the role or responsibility of employers to provide the meaning in our lives. However, I do believe that what's important is for employers to provide the playground in which employees have the potential to find the best version of themselves and to achieve something meaningful.

If, for example, you have worked in many departments and tried many roles within an organization, from customer service to marketing—and you still can't find anything anywhere that turns you on—then very possibly you need to move on from that company in order to find the best version of yourself and discover meaning and purpose in your life.

You need to be able to answer questions like:

- How am I doing in relation to how I could operate in the world?
- Does my life make sense?
- Is this who I am?
- Am I being the best version of myself?
- Is this where I'm supposed to be at this age?
- How do I compare to other people of my age?
- Am I heading in the right direction?
- Is this going to get me where I want to get to?

Finding meaning is ultimately about discovering answers to three very simple questions:

Who am I?

Why am I here?

What am I supposed to do now that I am here?

The questions are really no more complicated than that!

As we increase our consciousness, what we are saying is that we are developing a greater understanding of who we are, what drives us, what motivates us, what our values are, what our strengths are, what makes us tick, what turns us on.

That new understanding and self-awareness will help us make more considered decisions and choices.

The benefit of this BREAKTHROUGH for me personally was enormous. I became completely focused on doing something I am good at, something I love, and something that allows me to be the very best version of myself. It also pays the bills—and makes a difference. I feel in FLOW! in The Zone.

Find your own . . . unique . . . personal . . . North Star!

Breakthrough #2

Determine Your Destiny by the Decisions You Make

Our supercomputer brain constantly waits for our next command. It's capable of processing 30 billion bits of information in just one second along its 6,000 miles of wiring and cabling. The 28 billion neurons in our bodies that make our supercomputer work can also each process one million bits of information per second through the 100,000 miles of nerves wired into our bodies. Pretty cool, eh?

So, with all of this massive computing firepower at our disposal, you would think we could have figured out how to be happy, wouldn't you? And that the combined brainpower of seven billion of us would have found some solutions to end hunger and poverty by now, not to mention, bring about world peace!

Less than 10 percent of people who buy a self-help book ever read past the first chapter. So if you've made it this far, your "best version of yourself" will definitely thank you! Have you noticed how most people (somewhat defensively!) claim that they know exactly what it is that they need to do in order to live a great life? And that they don't need you or me or anyone else telling them anything different!

However, KNOWING isn't enough. We must DO. Sadly, few people ever do what they know.

And before we DO, there is the massively important step of DECIDING.

In 1954 Roger Bannister DECIDED he would break the four-minute-mile record—and he did. Within just a year 37 others also broke it. His decision empowered others to achieve greatness, too.

In the Wheel of Life model, the MENTAL SPOKE is about learning and knowing. Learning about ourselves, knowing what we need to do to become the very best version of ourselves, and then, having processed all this, making a DECISION, a mental act of commitment, to do something about it.

Whether it's emotional mastery or financial mastery or physical mastery or relationship mastery that you seek, unless you DECIDE and DO something about it, nothing will change.

Information brings power and mastery only when it's acted upon.

And repetition is the mother of mastery. So make decisions often. The mind is a muscle—and underuse will impair its ability and strength. Use it or lose it!

Since **our decisions determine our Destiny**, we had also better choose wisely. (More on this in BREAKTHROUGH #6)

What eventually arises from enough repetition is DEEP KNOW-HOW or wisdom—often, a simple intervention, strategy, capability or belief—and the second we "get it," it can be applied to make our lives better.

However, in the meantime, there is often so much conflicting and confusing stuff out there—and inside us—that it's hard to know where to start.

To learn easily, take new information on board and make wise decisions, it's helpful to understand how decisions get made.

Our brains have a process for making decisions. It's driven by "programming" in our subconscious minds, which acts like some invisible force, directing all of our actions, feelings and choices—both good and bad.

This subconscious program was installed without our knowledge or permission by parents and previous generations, teachers, siblings, playmates, peers, TV, advertisers, the media, politicians and our culture.

The program has four operating processes:

Our stories: This includes our beliefs about life, its rules–and our worldview.

Our values: This includes what we hold dear.

Our context: This includes our reference points.

Our emotions: This includes our fears, how we experience things–and the questions this raises for us.

In addition, we are designed to make choices so as to GAIN PLEASURE or AVOID PAIN. Sadly, for most people, the fear of loss or pain is much greater than the desire for gain or pleasure. And because we are all different, what causes pain or pleasure is different for everyone.

But we can control our life–rather than allowing it to control us. We can choose to gain pleasure, rather than to avoid pain–to move toward gain, rather than moving away from pain. This understanding is essential if we want to change our behaviors, as what we link to pain and gain shapes our DESTINY.

In order to succeed at changing anything, we must have LONG-TERM FOCUS as well as SHORT-TERM FOCUS.

Most of the problems or painful experiences we face in life, from cashflow challenges and relationship conflicts, to overindulging in food or alcohol, come from short-term focus problems. The failure lies in lack of control over what we focus on, the failure to manage our mental and emotional states–and failure in persistence and follow-up.

Long-term success, however, is the result of making lots of great small decisions that result in being the very best version of ourselves. It's deciding to feed our own mind, rather than allowing it to be fed externally by the media or others telling us what we need or how we should be.

Look around and see everywhere in business and society how our short-term instant gratification and quick-fix focus creates long-term problems.

Mental strength is required to make long-term focus decisions that will set you on the right course to achieve your dreams and become the best version of yourself.

Choose to MOVE TOWARD what you DECIDE to DO, rather than to move away from what you don't want to do.

Making better decisions and changing our behaviors leads us to better outcomes. However, the Mental Spoke is not just about decisions but also our BELIEFS—achieving BREAKTHROUGHs also requires us to change our BELIEFS.

It's not the events of our lives that shape us. It's the BELIEFS we have about the meaning of those events.

A case study done on twin girls raised by a prostitute, drug-addicted single mother, showed that they grew up to be quite different. One became a prostitute, drug-addicted single mother—the other a nurse, wife and mother with an educated, happy family. When asked how that happened, they both replied, "How else could my life have developed, given the way I was brought up?"

The different beliefs they held determined the outcomes for them, as well as making the difference between happiness and destitution.

Sadly, most people are too busy making excuses for themselves and so the bar isn't set that high. And all of their excuses are BS (Belief Systems!).

You will always get what you believe—and resonate with—manifesting either pain or pleasure. This is WavePower in action (more on this in BREAKTHROUGH #10).

So it's important to decide on what I call **Minimum Acceptable Standards.** If you don't, you'll slip into behaviors and attitudes that are so much lower than are available to you.

People don't miss out on a great life because of their education, or the way their parents treated them, or the neighborhood they grew up in. They have the life they have because that's what they have chosen—and what they believe. It's that simple.

When Rosie, my daughter, was four years old, I went to listen to Christmas carols at her kindergarten in the little nursery school next to where we lived. All the children were gathered at the front of the stage, the teacher and the parents around the outside.

The teacher said to all the children, "Hands up, those of you who can sing," and every child in the group put their hand up.

When the teacher turned around to the parents and said, "Hands up, those of you who can sing," only three people put their hand up.

She said, "What is it that happens between the age of four and the age of thirty-four that somehow makes us think we can't sing?"

We adults had lost the belief that we could sing, while those children all innately believed that they could.

What happens as we mature is that people turn around and say, "You've got a lousy voice. Don't sing." Or, "You sound terrible," and we end up believing it.

If we're not aware, we can become vulnerable to negative and conflicting beliefs from society and the world that stick—but that have nothing to do with who we really are. The BREAKTHROUGH of living as the best version of Self, at our highest potential, requires that we "unlearn," as Yoda would say in the movie *Star Wars*, what we have learned from other people.

Our teachers, our parents, our society and our media, all tell us we're not "luminous beings." So we start to believe that we are inadequate. We start to believe that we are incomplete. We start to believe that we're not glamorous, gorgeous, tall, sporty, intelligent, smart or wealthy enough. But enough for what?

From the age of four—and for the rest of our lives—society can metaphorically take away from us our "ability to sing." Or at least, it can if we let it, if we don't wake up, change the story and say to ourselves, "You know what? I can sing and even if no one else likes my singing, I do!"

Learn from the decisions that you've made in the past—but don't be imprisoned by them.

I brought up my two children on my own for most of the 18 years prior to them leaving home, aged 25 and 21. I loved them equally, provided for them equally, guided and parented them equally. But they are as different as chalk and cheese. They make different choices about the way things are and how they want to be. They have different beliefs about what's possible and what they need to put in to achieve what they want. They will both create their own self-fulfilling prophecy. They will likely end up in quite different places with divergent worldviews. I find this hard to handle sometimes, but my philosophy of parenting is to teach them to fish rather than give them fish, and so I aim to be their role model, rather than dictate what their "best" beliefs or behavior should be.

Our beliefs are no more than a feeling of conviction and certainty that can appear "real" to us. With enough emotional intensity ("charge") and repetition, our mind and nervous system "imagines" and experiences what's happening as real, even if it hasn't happened yet.

Belief and imagination are qualities that differentiate leaders from the rest—leaders are not realistic. They are smart and canny, but by others' standards they are not realistic. They imagine future states and then make them reality. It's the difference between "I believe it, therefore I see it" versus "I see it, therefore I believe it."

New experiences only change outcomes if they cause us to change our beliefs, too. This is why changing beliefs alone, or behaviors alone—rather than both together—will not achieve a BREAKTHROUGH.

Sadly, the system makes us believe that we are all incomplete in some respect (advertising being the worst offender).

Learned helplessness is the condition that most people live in. They believe "nothing will get better" or "it's all pointless" or "it doesn't matter what I do, it won't make any difference" or, worse, "I am worthless."

And at the same time, anyone they perceive to be ahead of them in terms of completeness is perceived as a threat—and they want to knock him or her off the pedestal.

So many people live in fear of loss—losing their job, their home, a loved one, their income, status or health—which feeds a strong sense of insecurity.

We are not totally created by our circumstances—our circumstances are created by us.

Learned helplessness robs us of personal power and of our ability to act.

I have stopped worrying about maintaining the quality of my life because I have replaced this with working each day on IMPROVING it.

The only security I now focus on in my life is the knowledge that every day I can improve myself in some way, however big or small. And because small wins are believable, they are also so much more achievable.

Each day I look for ways to expand. It's exciting living like that.

I have also learned the veracity of the phrase, "This too shall pass." And so, even in the middle of a storm, even when I can't understand how it happened or why I attracted it, I can always rely on the fact that it will pass and that the sun will shine again shortly.

It's how we deal with adversity more than anything else that will determine our DESTINY and shape our lives.

Although I now understand that my past failures and frustrations laid the foundations for the new level of living that I enjoy, it's what I decide to do with that knowledge from here on that will make the rest of my life meaningful and significant.

Only we can decide who and what we are committed to being and having in our lives.

Making no decision is, of course, a decision as well. It's making a choice to be directed by life rather than to create your own.

Until we DECIDE to raise our game, change our beliefs, and adopt new behaviors, we will never enjoy mastery.

It's time to decide how you are going to live the next ten years of your life.

But first, you need to decide how you will live TODAY, because the actions you take today will shape your FUTURE.

So on this, the first day of your journey to mastery, what do you stand for—"okay," "fine," "good," "great" . . . or "sensational"?

Whatever you decide will determine your ultimate DESTINY.

And by the way, your choice of words is critical in your decisions. The difference between being INTERESTED in an outcome and DECIDING on that outcome is the difference between night and day.

Saying things like:

"I'd like to earn more money."

"I'd like to have a better relationship with my partner."

"I'd like to have a better relationship with my kids."

. . . won't get you anywhere. They aren't commitments. They are wishes. There is no power or energy in such language.

One of the ways to achieve a BREAKTHROUGH in this area is to be alert to—and stop yielding to—any victim language.

If I tell myself, "I can't sing," I won't. If I tell myself, "I'm not strong enough to lift that spacecraft out of the swamp," I won't be able to. I'll give up and go and slump up the bank, like Luke Skywalker did. Even though he could clearly lift it out halfway, he then gave up.

The choice of words we apply to any given situation affects our mental state more than we realize. Choosing the right words makes us smile and changes our state.

A client once told me, "I cannot forgive." When I suggested he replace those words with, "I choose not to forgive," his whole body language changed and the expression on his face moved from one of deeply suppressed, unexpressed anger to one of freedom and relief.

If we want to shape our beliefs, our actions, our lives—and influence our DESTINY—we need to choose our words consciously. Selecting better words expands our possible outcomes.

If a phrase or sentence you regularly use disempowers you, replace it with one that empowers you.

Think of the difference between "I feel confused" versus "I'm curious," "exhausted" versus "recharging," "lost" versus "searching."

Shifting from the language of "being done to" can move us from victim mentality to "hero mentality."

Notice the step up from "I'm attractive" to "I am beautiful," or from "happy" to "ecstatic." We can shift from a good life to a great life, just through our choice of vocabulary.

I am often teased by people who ask, "How are you?" when we meet up in person or catch up on the phone, because my standard reply is, "Extremely well, thank you." If I choose to say I am extremely well, I feel extremely well. And if I feel extremely well, I make smarter choices and feel better about my life. It really works and it's that simple. Try it.

Our choice of vocabulary also plays a huge role in determining the quality of what we manifest and attract in both our current reality and our DESTINY.

Highly successful people have a vocabulary that is all about positive things: love, gratitude, curiosity, passion, determination, flexibility, confidence, vitality and happiness. Whereas losers tend to have a language that fixates on loneliness, overload, inadequacy, guilt, pain, disappointment, frustration, anger, fear, boredom and other negative things.

An added benefit of using better words is asking better questions. And the questions we ask determine what we think about.

Isn't that what thinking is? Asking and answering questions?

Great leaders I have worked with ask better, smarter questions than others. **Quality questions create a quality life. It's that simple.**

I know it's gotten me into lots of trouble over the years (and lots of success, too), but I look around and get so frustrated by people who, presented with a problem, ask, "Why me?" I prefer to look at the same set of circumstances and say, "Why not? Let's give it a go!"

If you ask a terrible question, you'll get a terrible answer. If you ask a great question, you'll get a great answer.

But it's the questions we fail to ask ourselves that also shape our DESTINY.

Our questions shape our perspective on who we are, what we are capable of, and what we are willing to invest in achieving our dreams. So, ask yourself empowering questions. Ask yourself new possibility-creating questions.

What am I happy about?

What am I excited about?

What am I proud of?

Who do I love?

Who loves me?

What have I been generous about?

Who have I helped?

What have I learned today?

How about these two questions?

What am I truly grateful for in my life right now?

Am I being the best version of myself?

I ask myself these two questions every single day. And, habitually, I ask myself the second question as often as possible while facing the hundreds of choices I make each day about how to be in the world.

I love questions like, "How can I learn from this and get a better outcome next time it happens?" and "How can I turn this around?" and "What are the positives in this situation?" and "How can this help me grow?"

We all have the same power at our disposal. We all have the ability to ask ourselves the same questions. And these questions determine our outcomes.

I used to love asking Rosie and Tom at bedtime, "What did you learn today?"

Their personalities shone through from such a young age in their answers. My favorite answer was one Tom gave when he was about nine. Instead of telling me what he had learned that day, he asked me, "Dad, ever since you have been a grown-up, have you ever needed to know how slowly glaciers move?"

I laughed out loud and said, "No, why do you ask?"

"Dad, why do they teach us this rubbish at school?"

"They are teaching you to learn," I replied.

"That's such a Dad answer!" he groaned.

Going back to that supercomputer brain of ours . . . every time we experience pain, our brain looks for the cause and records it, along with various other associations. Then, the next time a similar experience occurs, it remembers how to respond.

However, the programming of our past need not determine our future.

Thankfully, the same process applies with great pleasure—and equally, to emotions such as passion, courage, commitment and love, which can fade if not reinforced.

Experience is not what happens to us, it's what we do with what happens to us.

Success and wisdom are the result of good judgment. Good judgment is the result of experience . . . and experience is so often the result of poor judgment.

So remember to focus on what you choose—not what you fear. And focus on how you will achieve it.

So many people focus on avoiding rejection or anger, loneliness, guilt or humiliation. A man who chooses to pursue prosperity is much more likely to end up rich than a man who focuses on avoiding poverty.

Similarly, if we focus on avoiding war we will get war, whereas if we focus on creating peace we will achieve peace.

It's not good enough just to have a great mind. We have to use it. If we don't use it, we lose it. You snooze, you lose!

Using the power of decision gives you the ability to change any part of your life for the better. The minute you truly decide to change, your life will change. You can do almost anything you dream of.

There are just four simple steps:

- **Decide what you want**
- **Do something about it**
- **Focus—and adjust with a five-degree (5º) course correction where necessary**
- **Enjoy!**

And remember to be mindful of how you focus! A "determined" focus will cause things to happen much faster than relying on "luck"!

And focus on feeling happy, because at the end of the day, any change we ever want to make boils down to wanting to feel happier.

Despite that simple truism, sadly, most people cannot make a list of 100 things that make them happy. Can you?

I challenge you to put this book down and do it right now! (See TOOL #23.) And then pick one thing on your list—and commit.

I have tried and tested every BREAKTHROUGH in this book, on myself and with clients, and they work. But without commitment to the DECISION to do something with them, this, and all the others, are worthless.

Once you commit to something, take action.

Nothing will happen without a decision, so you might as well make it consciously and wisely—and be committed to it.

I have figured out from experience that there is always a way to turn a situation around if I decide to do so and I am committed.

To be committed, I need to feel and be responsible. I need to believe that something must change, and that I can and must change it.

There are no failures in life. Just results.

Stick to your decisions—and at the same time check regularly what's working—and always remain flexible. If you don't get the results you want, learn from what you have accomplished and then course-correct until you do get the outcome you want.

It's not what you did in the past that will determine your future, or even what you are doing right now—it's what you DECIDE to do next. It's in these "crucible" moments that our destiny is determined.

People who make it and succeed in life demonstrate a never-ending commitment to act until they achieve. They decide how much they want to earn, where they want to live, who they want to hang out with, and what toys and activities they want to reward themselves with. They are specific and proactive. They decide and commit. They reinforce each decision with empowering language and empowering thoughts.

They act "as if." They are the change they want to see in their lives. They are powerful beyond measure.

And all of that is the result of a decision. A consistent choice. If what they are doing doesn't work and achieve for them what they want, they try some other way to achieve the desired goal. They are relentless.

They have what I call a **Move Mountains Mental Menu.** (See TOOL #28.)

The only items on the menu are positive empowering thoughts and choices.

In the Move Mountains Mental Menu, you use only positive words and language. You focus only on positive MOVE TOWARD goals and reject any thoughts about moving away from negatives. You decide that everything you do will be positive, proactive and empowering—you set it up that way and act on it that way, in word and deed.

When we make these positive mental menu items into habits, these habits, in turn, create a positive us, demanding empowering emotions, enriching thoughts and powerful questions. We create new habits, new standards, new expectations, and new self-belief in our power to create the life we choose.

I promise that if you commit to using this BREAKTHROUGH TOOL, within a month you will have a completely different life—just from this one idea. You will attract positive people into your life who have positive ideas and opportunities for you to get involved with. You will attract the resources you need to implement your dreams and you will feel powerful beyond measure.

Another daily discipline to include is to feed your mind by reading. Leaders are readers. They are constant learners. They have the attitude that the day they stop learning is the day they start dying. They read to expand their minds and their worldview. They read to increase their vocabulary and their Move Mountains Mental Menu. It's a commitment to a constant sense of curiosity and a passion for growth and learning that sets apart the best from the rest.

And none of this is hard. None of this is complicated. None of this costs money.

Increasing our knowledge increases our awareness. People who know more have a better way of evaluating what their options are and so make smarter and better-informed choices.

All decisions we make are a reflection of our values, and our values determine the quality of our lives. We must be clear what's important in our lives and what's nonnegotiable, and decide to live in accordance with our values, no matter what happens. (See BREAKTHROUGH #8.)

If we stretch ourselves to a new higher level of living, we will never shrink back to our earlier dimensions.

Having a mentor can be invaluable when it comes to the decisions we need to make to become the best version of ourselves—and to stretch ourselves. A great mentor can guide you down the river, help you make the best choices at the forks, and help steer you through the rapids, past the boulders and over the falls.

My identity isn't defined by my experiences—it's defined by my attitude to who I am, and what I've decided to do. The same applies to you.

I know that the planet we live on is only one of several hundred million stars in our galaxy—and that our galaxy is only one of several hundred thousand million galaxies in our universe—and that on our planet, I am only one of seven billion humans. But I don't feel insignificant. I feel that I can make a difference, and I have decided that there is no better place for me to make a difference than right here, right now. And the best way I have discovered to make that difference is by being **THE MENTOR**— finding the boundaries of what's possible for myself—and others—and going beyond those boundaries into what others often consider to be impossible. It's a journey, where we . . . **"Feel the fear and do it anyway."**

Where we . . .

"Count not the breaths we take in our lives, but the moments in life that take our breath away."

I have decided I am competent to do almost anything—and that gives me the confidence to have a go. I see myself as a creator of possibilities, a catalyst for personal mastery, a fun-maker, a mentor, a dad, a partner, a friend, a teacher, a writer (well, now at least!), a speaker, a networker and connector, a healer, a challenger, M : A : D (Making A Difference), outrageous . . . and modest.

I have decided to identify with the highest parts of me, and to simply recognize certain other areas as ones that I am still working on in order to become the best version of myself. Rather than focus on flaws in my character, I focus on areas and opportunities for growth.

The following are some of the M : A : D decisions I live by.

Decide to give it your best shot, to experiment and take the risk to change

Decide to consume only a Move Mountains Mental Menu

Decide to do something every day for someone who can never repay you

Decide to be grateful for all of the positive things that happen in your life

Decide to play the game of life . . . and

Decide to win.

What M : A : D decisions do you choose to live by?

Breakthrough #3

To Infinity–
and Beyond!

To me, life has to be a daring adventure or it's not worth living.

Too many people live life unconsciously, taking whatever fork in the river "goes with the flow," but then realize further downstream that they did indeed have a choice at that last fork, and for some reason made the choice to make "no choice."

If you don't shape your own future, guess what? Someone else will!

I love the scene in the movie *Alice in Wonderland* when Alice arrives at the crossroads and sees the Cheshire Cat up in the tree. She asks the cat where a particular road she points to will lead her. The Cheshire Cat inquires where she is headed. Alice replies, "Well, it doesn't really matter." Wisely, the Cheshire Cat says, "In which case it doesn't really matter which road you take."

It's not that if you continue life's journey unconsciously you will necessarily have a "bad" life. Indeed, you could well end up by many standards having a "good" one. But in the words of Jim Collins, "Good is the enemy of great." And what we are after is the BEST version of you, not a mediocre version! So, good is not good enough for you. We want a BREAKTHROUGH to GREAT!

To start with, we need a VISION. A destination.

I know, I know. I hear you saying, "Success is the journey, isn't it? Not the destination." Well, yes! But it really is so much better if directionally we are headed somewhere that we have chosen to go, to become a better version of ourselves, rather than aimlessly drifting through life headed nowhere in particular.

How do organizations inspire their employees to be more than observers, to actively create their own futures? Vision.

How do parents do the same with their children? I believe, in the same way. Vision.

Having a positive vision of the future is the most powerful motivator for change that companies, schools, communities, nations, and individuals possess.

This is why great leaders inspire the people in their organizations to think together, dream together, and act together to make a difference by:

- Creating a compelling vision that goes beyond numbers
- Inspiring others to stretch beyond their perceived limits

Having a positive vision of the future is what gives meaning to our present life.

Most people, sadly, dabble their way through life and fail to achieve their potential simply because they major in minor things.

I've come to believe that once we've made a decision and then focus or concentrate our power as a vision, it's like generating a laser beam of energy that can blast through walls and accomplish for us anything we set our minds to.

Six months or so before my 40th birthday, I saw an advertisement for a one-day personal development "visioning" workshop that caught my attention. The offer was to "create the life you have always dreamed of." What's more, this one-day seminar, which was being held the following Saturday, cost only $50—so I figured I had nothing to lose and phoned to sign up immediately!

Just a few days later, I arrived at the town hall in a country village close to where I lived. It was a gorgeous summer day. The room was huge, and in the middle were four workstations arranged in a square. Each workstation had two easels with a large (poster-size) piece of white paper resting horizontally. In front of the easels was a table with two massive piles of identical magazines, scissors, glue and crayons.

Our facilitator gave us instructions, and by the end of the workshop, I had created two boards—a TODAY BOARD and a DREAM BOARD—or as I now prefer to call it, a GOALS POSTER.

By the way—if you want to undertake this exercise for yourself—you'll find it in the BREAKTHROUGH RETREAT WORKBOOK TOOL #21. I've chosen to change the name, because for me a "goal" has more power and action behind it than a "dream" does.

Toward the end of the workshop, each of the participants was asked to explain their TODAY BOARD and where they were at present in their lives—and then share their DREAM BOARD. I was impressed by how clear they all were about what they wanted and how they intended to get there.

I waited until last, feeling embarrassed about how my poster had turned out—and worse, how little clue I had about where I really wanted to end up in my life, and what success looked like for me. I was ashamed at how shallow and stupid it all looked—and also felt—when it was my turn to explain my efforts to the group.

Given my profession as a mentor, I was also appalled by how not "together" my TODAY life was compared to my fellow participants. Something big needed to change!

Interestingly, at the conclusion of the exercise, there was still a small pile of photos I'd cut out that hadn't been stuck onto either board. The teacher was intrigued by these and asked me about them. I genuinely didn't have any idea why I had cut these particular items out.

As we spread them out on the table, the teacher honed in on a picture of a gold watch, questioning me about what it meant to me. I explained that this was something I didn't want in my life, but felt society projected that I "should" have if I was to be seen as successful.

Eureka! We had cracked the code. I had cut out images of a bunch of items representing what I felt society wanted me to be, do and have—and that I was resisting.

Anyway, overall, it was pretty clear to everyone in the room—including me—that I had absolutely no clue whatsoever about what my Dream Life really looked like—nor any idea how to achieve it.

This was a huge shock to me, as I'd always seen myself as such a dynamic person, forging my way ahead in life.

The truth revealed in doing this exercise was that I was heading nowhere in particular. My life was a series of hedonistic experiences without any direction or aim or purpose.

I also realized that I spent a huge amount of time doing things for others, and that of the few personal life goals that I was able to identify, most involved, or even depended upon, other people.

At the end of the workshop, as I was about to head home, feeling humiliated, deflated and confused—the teacher stopped me.

He said, "If you had six months to complete this exercise again, how different would it look?"

"Very different," I replied.

"Would you like to do it again and get together when you feel it reflects what's deep in your heart—and your Dream Life?"

"Yes, please," I replied.

Several months later, I had completely reworked my 40th birthday TODAY BOARD—and also created my 50th birthday GOALS POSTER.

I invited the teacher over for supper and went through them with him.

Instead of continuing to wander through life like *Alice in Wonderland*, I now had a very clear picture of what success looked like—and what the best version of me looked like—physically, spiritually, mentally, emotionally, personally and professionally.

Following that experience, I had so many realizations about previous times where I had not made choices wisely. Now that I had created a map of where I was heading, I could make smarter, better choices to achieve my Goals.

I created a screensaver for my computer from a photo of the GOALS POSTER that served as a daily reminder of my Goals.

I began to make much more discerning choices about who I spent time with, where I spent time and what I spent time doing. My Goals began to show up faster—and in ways that were smarter—than I had ever thought possible.

Five years later, when we were about to move house, my son, Tom, found my GOALS POSTER in the attic. He brought it downstairs, dusted it off and showed it to me. I nearly fell off my chair.

"Look, Dad, we have been here—and here—and here! You have done this—and this—and that. You've got that car! We're moving to that town next week! Rosie and I go to that school! You've opened your office in New York!" . . . and so on.

Despite it originally being a ten-year GOALS POSTER, I had already achieved every single goal on the board.

Strangely, for a few weeks prior to that experience, I'd been saying things to myself like, "It's time for a move, a new location, a new way of living!" I had even admitted to myself one day that I was a bit bored. Now I realized why—it was my lack of goals and hence, striving to become a better version of myself, that was causing me frustration.

I now do the GOALS POSTER exercise with all of my clients—and I also do it for myself approximately every two or three years.

Something interesting occurred while doing my last one. By my 53rd birthday, I had already accomplished everything on the GOALS POSTER I'd created a few years earlier and was keen to start a new one. However, because I now KNOW that when I put something on the board IT WILL HAPPEN, I noticed that it was taking much longer than usual to complete the new poster.

Much of my uncertainty had to do with where and how I really wanted to live. After four months, I finally found a photo of an apartment that "fit"—40th floor, great views! However, as it turned out, I would only be able to move into this development when it was completed and ready for occupancy—which was some two years hence! The savings campaign started that day!

The GOALS POSTER exercise has become one of my favorite tools to use for myself and with others. It focuses and gives power to our most daring decisions. It's a way of committing to them—and reminding ourselves of them everyday.

All you need to begin (aside from the materials), is whatever is PRESENT in your life in this moment—and you just build from there.

Please remember to also apply BREAKTHROUGH #2 when creating your GOALS POSTER, as my experience has been that if you focus on it—and resonate with it—you will manifest it!

Just one final piece of advice with this BREAKTHROUGH . . .

Please be careful what you wish for!

Breakthrough #4

Only Do What Only You Can Do

When I begin working with new clients, I take them away for two days to do a retreat. During those two days we unpack who they are and what they do as leaders. One of the exercises we undertake as part of this two-day onboarding retreat is to look at how they manage their time.

We print out the previous six months and future six months from their diaries and take out four different-colored highlighter pens.

The first highlighter pens I give them are the red ones. I ask them to go through their diaries in the last six months and highlight the things that absolutely should have been deleted, were a complete waste of their time, the company's time, the company's money, other people's time and money, and just should simply not have happened. People, activities, whatever.

So they go through the previous six months and very often make the comment, "Gosh, that's an awful lot of red highlighter."

I then hand them orange highlighters and ask them to go through again and highlight the things which someone else in their organization could or should have done, and they should have delegated.

We then write down the percentage of time that could or should have been deleted or delegated.

Generally speaking, by the time they've finished this exercise, they're feeling pretty sick in the stomach. Why? Because usually 50 percent or more of their time has been spent on things that either should have been deleted from their diaries or should have been delegated.

I then hand them yellow highlighter pens and ask them to highlight the things where they were learning, growing, developing and preparing themselves for the next stage.

In practice, there are very rarely any yellow highlighted items.

And finally I hand them green pens and I ask them to highlight the times when they were being the very best versions of themselves, when they were flying high, playing to their strengths, absolutely *in THE ZONE*, and they were the only person in their organization who could have done what they were doing at that point in time.

And, thankfully, they all have a few areas like that which they highlight. I ask them, "How did you feel when you were doing that? *Why* were you *in The Zone* then?"

Those times that they identify with the green highlighter—those times when they were the only person in their organization who could do what they did—those are invariably the times for which they're really being paid.

I ask, "If you could fill up your week with green things, when you're only doing what only you can do, which is to be the great inventor, to be the great creative, to be the great sales person, to be the great visionary or motivator, and you can delete or delegate all the other things that are filling up your diary, how much of a BREAKTHROUGH would that achieve in your own life, and how would that impact on the results of your organization?"

They "get it" straightaway, and realize that it would be an enormously important BREAKTHROUGH for them. And for their businesses.

This process of adopting an analytical approach to your schedule is hardly rocket science. How could it be, when it involves a technology no more sophisticated than four differently colored highlighter pens?

But if we can achieve a potential major BREAKTHROUGH, just by focusing harder on what we do with our time and by making the enormously important decision to maximize the hours we spend on doing those things that only we can do, doesn't this suggest that there must be many other areas of our lives where we can achieve scarcely less momentous BREAKTHROUGHs?

What I then do is ask my clients to look at the next six months that they already have planned in their diaries. The people I mentor tend to be super-busy and to have their time booked up well in advance. I then ask them to apply the same process, involving the colored pens, to the next six months of their schedule that haven't happened yet.

What kinds of responses do I typically get when I do this?

Well, what happens is that these people are startled by how much of the stuff in their diaries is activity that could be deleted from their schedules, and maybe should be, as it doesn't involve them doing things that only they could be doing.

Typically they tell me, "If you hadn't pointed this out, I'd have just carried on and wasted much of my time on stuff that I should be delegating or deleting. From now on I'm going to be focusing on areas where I am going to be the best version of myself."

There's a lesson here that applies to everyone, not only people running major international organizations. The lesson is that the more we are able to focus on doing those things that make the best use of our unique skills—I mean those things that make us feel that we are now being the very best versions of ourselves—the more likely it is that our personal and professional lives will be replete with BREAKTHROUGHs.

Breakthrough #5

Attitude Determines Altitude

In the same way that the Chinese character for "crisis" (below) comprises the signs for both "danger" and "opportunity," I refuse to accept that there's such a thing as "disaster." Rather, I subscrlbe to the idea that anything that doesn't kill you is an opportunity to learn.

When I'm looking at a complex or sad situation, I often wonder, what on earth the opportunity to learn might be in this situation?

Like most people, I've been through some pretty jolting and difficult experiences in my life—divorces, business relationships, a difficult relationship with my dad, virtually going bankrupt in business and nearly going personally bankrupt as a result, and I was a single parent for 16 years. I've had some very difficult things to deal with.

But, you know, if you talk to elderly people and ask them to look back on their lives, they always tell you their war stories. They always tell you the things that went wrong and that they overcame. They always tell you about the scrapes and the narrow misses.

These are the things they are most proud of because these are the things that they learned the most from—the things that eventually turned them into the people they became.

Several years ago I interviewed numerous candidates who were all extremely successful and highly respected former CEOs of major multinationals, all in their fifties. They had all reached "The Winners' Enclosure." I was interviewing them to be a mentor in my old firm. Anyone who sat there and told me, "Well, I've never made a mistake in my career and I've never done anything wrong," was instantly eliminated as a potential mentor. How could they possibly understand a normal Chief Executive who had difficulties at home and at work all day, every day, to deal with?

The greatest gift in my life was being a single parent. I learned more about being a man, about being David C. M. Carter, about life and unconditional love, from being a single father than anything else could ever have taught me. And I didn't ever regret it or curse it.

Did I think it would be of such benefit when it happened at the time? No, I didn't, but it still turned out to be the greatest gift I've ever received.

I have been married a few times, all real gifts. I've learned so much.

I've been involved in many businesses over the years—some have been really successful, some have worked out okay, and one or two haven't worked out very well at all. Again, real gifts, and every one has been an opportunity for learning.

The point in sharing these experiences is this—whatever happens to you in your life, you need to stop and ask yourself a very simple question: **What am I willing to take responsibility for in this situation?**

I absolutely believe, without any doubt whatsoever, that the great challenges we face in our lives are what make us most human, most alive.

Today, whenever someone says in a mentoring session, "Oh my God, it's a disaster! Oh my God, this has happened!" and wants to talk about it, it doesn't take me more than half an hour to get that person to see all the positives.

The point is, there's always an equal and opposite positive to every negative. It's not that the disaster doesn't exist. The negative, the pain, the hurt, the sadness, may all be present—but there is an equal and opposite emotion going on as well that we choose, in a moment of crisis, not to look at, not to talk about.

And if you talk to people who have been through business challenges, relationship dilemmas, health issues, whatever, after the event, they will always tell you the good that they eventually realized came from it.

When we learn and grow, we never regret the things we did. When we learn and grow, we only ever regret the things we didn't do.

And the most unfortunate events, that may at first seem like setbacks from which one can never recover, may in fact come to be seen as positively beneficial.

If you ask people a year after they've lost their job, or a relationship ended, or they had to give up the sport they enjoyed because of an injury, whether any good came of it, they will say things like:

> "Well, I wouldn't have had a chance to meet this person . . . "

> "I wouldn't have had a chance to spend time reading and learning about this new exciting thing . . . "

> "I wouldn't have had time to sort out this part of my life . . . "

> "I actually realized that for years I had been doing X and I really hadn't been enjoying it. Now I'm doing Y and I'm loving it."

So invariably, when you say to them, "What was the good that came out of it?" they've all got something positive to say about every experience.

You might not be able to see it at the time, but at the exact same point in time that something bad is happening to you, something good is happening, too.

As you become more conscious, you can close the time gap between what you perceive at the time to be negative and what you see later as positive. We have this fixed view that things are either good or bad in life, when in fact they are always both.

For example, I know now that for many years in one business I was involved with, I kept trying to do something that actually was impossible. And I thought, "I'll try this way . . . I'll try that way," and I went on for six or seven years persevering with something that wasn't ever going to work.

So what did I get out of all this? Did I fail? No, I figured out that I have perseverance, stamina and ambition. I saw the positives. I realized I'd learned something and went on to set up my own mentoring business, embracing the lessons learned.

Similarly, in personal relationships it is often the case that one must sometimes go through an extremely difficult time in order to reach the "sunny uplands" of a true and deep friendship. Most of us at some time in life experience the agony of lost love. What I have learned now is that **grief is about the loss of the relationship I had hoped for, not the one I actually had.**

Being hurt and recovering from the hurt, and finding that it has spiritually enriched us and deepened us to an extent that we very likely would not have believed possible, is one of the supreme human experiences.

Taking every step to avoid such a hurt, or simply trying to be someone who is completely invulnerable to hurt or mishap, and who never makes a mistake, compromises the Self to such a terrible extent that we might as well not be alive at all.

Part of being human means exposing ourselves to the risks of life—and that means emotional risks, too. And sometimes we will get hurt. But we should always be kind to ourselves. If we are hurt emotionally, we should remember that a new love will come along—even if we find that hard to believe at first.

Life is more generous to us than we sometimes realize. Stay positive, hold on to your own thoughts regarding what is helpful and kind and generous, and life will reward you and make you realize you already are, and always were, whole. And soon you will feel fully alive again.

Breakthrough #6

Always Do the Right Thing and Do It the Right Way

Karma works.

We reap what we sow.

You get what you give.

What goes around comes around.

Like attracts like.

You must be the change you wish to see in the world.

There are so many ways of saying the same thing, commonly referred to these days as "The Law of Attraction."

Ignore this Universal Law at your peril.

One aphorism even goes so far as to suggest . . .

Be nice to folks on the way up, as you may need them on the way down.

I don't think I can recall one mishap in my life when, with hindsight, I either didn't have a "feeling" it might go wrong or a "feeling" that I was "getting away with something."

Hindsight is perfect 20:20 vision if we look hard enough.

And when I have gone wrong in my life, I can always point to the cause as being one item from a simple list. Take your pick from:

I didn't decide responsibly

I didn't decide wisely

I didn't decide—someone else decided for me

I didn't decide fearlessly

I didn't decide happily

I didn't decide compassionately

I didn't decide "without exits"

As we know from BREAKTHROUGH #2 we need to be willing to make decisions. That's probably the single most important ingredient in leadership. Leadership of others and leadership of self are crucial in order to live the life you dream of.

You have the ability to be a great leader, and like all great leaders, that means having the ability to do "unreasonable" things, such as the ability not to hear or be distracted by negative thoughts or emotions. Most unreasonable people succeed because they don't pay attention to how things can't be done.

Leadership requires two critical components. The first is belief from followers. The second is self-belief.

I am convinced that this is about doing the right thing and doing it the right way.

Doing the right thing and doing it the right way aren't easy. There are always easier, quicker, cheaper, more expedient ways of doing everything. But we all know that the other way is purely temporary and a Band-Aid faute de mieux solution.

This BREAKTHROUGH offers a new way of approaching these decisions.

To make the right decisions about the future and to do the right things the right way, we first need to take responsibility for a few things.

"I am where I am. I got here by being me and doing what I did. By accepting responsibility for my PAST, I free myself up to change gear and make a bigger, better FUTURE for myself."

Not only must we accept responsibility for our PAST and our PRESENT, we must also accept full responsibility for our FUTURE. The buck stops right here! With us!

Once we become competent in accepting responsibility for our PAST and our PRESENT, we must then take responsibility for implementing the "rules" for our FUTURE, by eliminating the word "will." This is how we create our reality—and our DESTINY.

> **I will always think and speak positively**

> **I will always act ethically**

I ~~will~~ always act with honor and respect

I ~~will~~ live my life as a statement of who I am

I ~~will~~ surround myself with like-minded people

I ~~will~~ make decisions and commit to them

I ~~will~~ face adversity fearlessly

I ~~will~~ always choose to be the best version of me

I ~~will~~ own my power

If I fail, it's because of my choices and decisions. No one else's.

Along with responsibility, we need to add **deciding wisely.**

Actively seeking wisdom to assist us in creating lives of extraordinary achievement is a sign of great strength.

Accepting that we can't change the past but can CHOOSE our future suggests that new ideas and new ways of thinking and seeing the world can only enhance our existing repertoire of skills.

. . . .

I have chosen not to watch television for more than 25 years now. I know that there are probably some great shows, but most of it looks to me like mindless rubbish. Yet I have not put down one self-help book in the 500-plus that I have read during the course of the last 15 years and thought, "What mind-numbingly moronic rubbish." There was always something new to learn and take on board as well as some old gems worth being reminded of.

In the same way that I choose carefully what I read, I choose equally carefully who I spend time with. I seek wisdom in what I read and I seek wisdom in my friends. I will only ever be a reflection of my friends. If I think my friends are stupid or lazy or mediocre, then so will you. As they say, we judge a man by the company he keeps.

If I hunt with chickens, I will spend my life scratching around looking in the dirt. If I hunt with eagles, I can stretch my wings and soar on the thermals to great heights. I choose to be an eagle and to listen to their counsel and wisdom.

I feel so blessed to have the friends I have, and I feel humbled and privileged to learn and grow from and with them.

I have noticed how many wealthy successful people are still modest, humble, polite, curious and interested. The wisdom they seek is available to all of us. It's just that winners take the time to collect it!

I have created my own WISDOM COUNCIL. It's like my own advisory board. I take problems and challenges and opportunities to them and run ideas past them to get their input before I press "PLAY."

I leverage their insights and contacts and ideas as well as learn from their experiences and intelligence. This has helped me both to make money and to close deals, and also to not waste money or lose deals on badly thought through ideas.

Who would you invite onto your own Advisory Board or Wisdom Council?

Others often don't understand this when I say it, but the people I learn the most from are my clients. Serving others as their mentor, valuing their wisdom and experiences and insights, adds value to my own wisdom and insights. And by generously sharing what I learned mentoring Client A on Monday with Client B on Tuesday, and so on, all my clients get to benefit from their collective wisdom.

Perhaps wisdom should be defined as "cool stuff remembered and passed on."

My personal credo has always been to "make yourself useful" and have an attitude of "How can I help you?" The desire to help others has been my greatest ever teacher and source of wisdom.

So, now that we have taken responsibility and decided wisely, it is time to decide to DO.

When faced with the choice of doing nothing (negative) or doing something (positive), I always choose to act and do something positive. Being a DO person is more than being a CAN DO or WILL DO person. Being a DO person means starting something NOW!

Carpe diem! Seize the day! Be courageous! History remembers the bold.

Create a wave of success and watch others step aside to let you through . . . then try and surf in your wake.

Successful people make decisions quickly and change their minds slowly. Losers make decisions slowly and change their minds quickly.

Heroes don't always win, but we remember their effort and the fact they gave it their all. We love seeing this in movies because it awakens us to the hero inside ourselves. Heroes don't always solve everything at once, but they always make a start and act with confidence.

Are you ready for success? Are you ready for your moment to be a hero? Have you decided what you will do when your moment arrives? What will you give up to get success? Will it be fears? Limiting beliefs? Time?

Success, like luck, happens when opportunity collides with preparedness.

Since we are all either in a crisis, have just come out of a crisis, or are potentially heading for a crisis, we should all accept that *challenge is part of being alive*. And if we are still here, there is still time. Time to fulfill our purpose.

Until you have accomplished what you came here to do, you are protected by the power of your purpose. As long as you are doing the right thing and doing it the right way, you will be successful.

Once you have decided to pull the trigger, the clarity of your vision is directly related to the effectiveness of your actions. Don't waver or have nagging doubts when others doubt your sanity or reasonableness. Victory is assured when you have made a decision and you stick to it.

Christopher Columbus spoke wisely when he said:

"Truth is truth. If a thousand people believe something foolish, it is still foolish! If they believe something true is foolish, it is still true! Truth is never dependent upon consensus of opinion. I have found that it is better to be alone and acting upon the truth in my heart than to follow a gaggle of silly geese doomed to mediocrity."

A wise man once said, "**A journey of a thousand miles begins with a single step.**" But most mediocre people stop walking when they face criticism, condemnation, complaint, humiliation or teasing and ridicule.

A bit like Christopher Columbus, we need the conviction to say to ourselves. "I have made my mind up. I have decided. I am passionate. I have a vision. Out of my way, please."

Or, in the words of Dr. Martin Luther King Jr.:

   "I have a dream!"

So what is your big dream? When will it come true? When will you take the first step? Who will you take on the journey?

A person without a dream never had a dream come true.

Resist any temptation to fail at what you want because of an undecided heart. Sure, you'll make a few wrong choices, which you will learn from, but go ahead and make decisions—and then make them right!

If it wasn't worth fighting and struggling for in the first place, your vision would be freely available to everyone without a struggle. Struggling makes you stronger.

If you are hunting for hares in hyena country, keep your eyes peeled for the hyenas. If you are just hunting for hyenas, you can ignore the hares.

If you want to win the lottery, you have to buy a ticket. If you want a great idea, you have to come up with lots of them. If you worry about others' opinions too much, you will have more confidence in their opinions than in your own ideas.

When a committed man encounters a problem, he searches for a solution. When a loser confronts a problem, he looks for an escape.

Burn your boat! Get passionate!

Passion breeds conviction and will turn mediocre into magnificent.

In the movie *Joan of Arc*, our heroine, a mere 17 years old, announced that she intended to strike at the heart of the barricade. Her captain advised her that no one would follow her. She replied:

"I won't be looking back!"

YES! Yes! Yes!

Start living life with a "just do it" attitude and ditch the more cautious, "Who? Me?" Replace any "Why?" with a "Why not?"

As Goethe said:

"Whatever you can do, or dream you can, begin it. Boldness has genius, power and magic in it."

Don't ask permission. Take it! Go! You will love it!

Being joyful is a choice. Deciding to be joyful will free your soul, and your spirit will soar.

Happiness is not a mystical, magical phantom floating in and around our lives. Happiness is a decision. A choice. Happiness is a chemical reaction to making the right decisions and doing things the right way. Happiness is an energy that, together with love, fuels the world. A great smile melts ice, heals broken hearts, and cements bonds.

Have you ever tried to be unhappy and grateful at the same time? It's impossible. Why? Because happiness comes from a grateful heart. Nothing negative can take root in a happy and gratitude-filled heart.

Expressing gratitude magnifies our happiness and attracts even more happiness.

Make a list of 100 things in your life that you are grateful for. Yes, 100! (See TOOL #22.)

When you have finished, you are guaranteed to feel happier than when you started writing the list!

. . . .

My dogs have been great teachers over the years. Every time I walked into the house, regardless of the time of day, how long I'd been away, the mood I was in, how tired or jet-lagged I was, Bella, my Border Collie, always greeted me as if it was her birthday and I'd given her the biggest and most important present ever. She shook her body and wagged her tail and panted with excitement. Seeing this, it took nanoseconds for me to be in a much happier frame of mind and my heart was immediately filled with happiness and gratitude.

Not to compare people to my dog but, when I think about it, my friends have the same effect on me. They make me feel wanted, warm, and welcome. As soon as I see them and reconnect, I feel safe and home and happy and joyful and pleased. I feel grateful and at peace.

It's no accident that "bella" means beautiful in Italian. So how do you make others feel more "bella"? Be more "bella" yourself!

Happiness and gratitude facilitate compassion and empathy.

Forgiving yourself for your past allows your spirit to flow free from baggage as it creates your desired future. Holding on to anger, as the Buddha once said, is like holding on to a hot rock that you want to throw at someone else. It only burns *your* hand. Holding on to anger or resentment or envy poisons your soul and limits your potential.

Forgiveness costs nothing. Forgiveness is worth millions. It's available to us all but used by so few. Forgiveness only has value when it's given. So the more you give, the freer you will feel.

Growing up, I faced many challenges in my relationship with my parents and felt I carried scars from the way I was raised.

However, when I forgave them and accepted that their parenting of me was the best version of them they were capable of at that time, compassion and forgiveness filled my heart. And as I directed this feeling toward my parents, I was also able to fill my heart with compassion and forgiveness for a few others in my life whom I felt had betrayed me.

By forgiving and feeling compassion for them, I released the demons that had been holding me prisoner and created a new horizon and a new future for myself. I was free.

I also noticed that I had a few stones in my shoes. Stones that didn't prevent me from walking, but prevented me from walking without pain or irritation. And those stones were people I hadn't forgiven for other, less serious misdemeanors. I forgave them, too. I forgave them even though they didn't ask for forgiveness. In truth, the stones were only ever in my shoes. They had been walking around oblivious to the pain they had caused me. I now feel completely free from past unproductive thoughts and baggage.

My hero, William Wilberforce, managed to abolish slavery in the British colonies. He did the right thing and he did it the right way. I realize now that I had been a slave to so many people, for so many years, who didn't even know I was imprisoned. I had enslaved and imprisoned myself. I am no longer a slave. I am free.

I forgive those who mock my dreams and criticize my goals. Who think I am too big for my boots. Too narcissistic. Too confident. I forgive their lack of vision, and forge ahead. I understand now that criticism is a price I have to pay for daring to be different and breaking away from mediocrity. I will not shrink in order to make others feel safe.

I want to do the right thing and I want to do it the right way. And I know I will be misunderstood and have detractors. I forgive them. I forgive myself. I do so because I have noticed that forgiveness affects me much more than it affects the person being forgiven.

Forgiveness is a decision, not an emotion. It's the ultimate antidote to anger.

You need a forgiving heart to be a great parent, friend, business partner, spouse, or trusted advisor.

Even if they don't ask for it, deserve it or need it—forgive them. Give it because it's ruining your life much more than it is theirs. Forgiveness is a gift you shower on yourself.

Seek to understand rather than condemn. Compassion only arises through empathy and understanding.

So, with that in mind, ask for forgiveness, too. It's an amazing experience.

I once went and apologized to more than twenty people who'd lost money on a deal I had put together. Eighteen of them made me shed a tear with the generosity of their comments and forgiveness. Only two were still angry. I forgave them, even though they didn't forgive me.

Even though someone might have done something terrible to you, forgive them—or the pain of remaining unforgiving will weigh you down forever. The release you will feel from forgiving them will set you free forever.

I love the story about the Native American elder mentoring his grandson and telling the tale of the fighting wolves. One wolf was full of anger, envy, sorrow, greed, arrogance, lies and ego. The other wolf was full of forgiveness. The young Native American warrior asked the elder, "Which wolf wins?" and his mentor replied, "The one I feed."

And finally, to achieve success in doing the right thing and doing it the right way, you need to be unreasonable and unrealistic.

Yes, that's right! Unreasonable and unrealistic.

Winners are never realistic by others' standards. They are never rational or logical or realistic or reasonable. There is a lesson in there somewhere, isn't there?

Such winners achieve success after success because they are somehow deaf and blind to what could go wrong. They persist. They have a "no exits" attitude.

The greatest gift I was ever given was the gift of choice. Today, I am persistent in pursuing my dreams and goals—not because I'm stubborn (although I think I can be sometimes!), but because I *choose* to pursue them. I choose this because I want to be the very best version of myself. And because I want to make a difference to help others. I want to do the right things and do them the right way.

Faith will always surpass reason as my lighthouse. And the reward of faith will be to live the life I have dreamed of and enjoy the journey it takes to get there.

I will persevere as long as required to achieve the desired results.

Persistence is a habit and it takes the same amount of energy as the habit of quitting or laziness.

Remember the local fairground? There is only a big prize for things that are hard to pull off and achieve. If it were easy, everyone would have hit the target or shot a bull's-eye, and the reward would be small.

And if you hit a wall, that's no reason to stop. It just means you need a new idea. That's all! A new idea.

Nothing in life is less important than the score at halftime. The tragedy of life isn't that we lose, it's that we nearly win.

Wherever you are at this point in your life, it's only halftime! You haven't lost, as the game isn't over yet. If you accept that the score at halftime will be the same as when the whistle blows, then you have already lost. So get out there and play your heart out in the second half and *go for it.* Do the right thing and do it the right way.

Breakthrough #7

Brand "You" . . . Your Personal Spoke

One of the questions that I ask all of my new clients early on in getting to know them is, "What's your personal brand?"

They can talk for hours and hours about the brands of the companies they lead and how that brand compares to other leading brands in their sector.

A few understand my actual question straight away (and have an answer), but most have never really considered it. Strangely, though, they immediately see its relevance—and why it's important that their "brand," or Personal Spoke, is a key part of what we work on together.

Of course, regardless of your age, position, or the business you happen to be in, we all have a brand already—whether we like it or not. And we need to understand the importance of that brand.

You are the CEO of your own global corporation—it's called **Brand You.**

And your most important job is to be CEO—and CMO—for **Brand You.**

The biggest fortunes being made in business these days are from small start-ups who get this brand BREAKTHROUGH correct and turn their great idea into a great IPO or exit in a short timeframe. They often notch up a phenomenal fortune by establishing their own micro equivalent of the Nike "swoosh." Think Skype, Facebook, Apple, Google, Twitter, etc.

So what can you learn from the big, famous brands that understand these fundamental principles? How might knowing something about these big, smart companies help you, too, to stand out and prosper—and be the very best version of yourself?

The great news is that everyone has the ability to stand out. Everyone has a chance to learn, improve, and build his or her capabilities. Everyone has a chance to be a brand worthy of note.

Highly recommended reading on this subject is a book called *Lovemarks* by Kevin Roberts—www.lovemarks.com. Check out some of the qualities he considers essential in branding—like Respect, Mystery, Sensuality and Intimacy.

Let's face it, these days, anyone can have a website. And today, because anyone can . . . anyone does! So how do we know which sites are worth visiting, which to bookmark, which are worth revisiting? The answer is—branding. The people and places we bookmark or return to are the ones we trust. Their brand is a promise of the value we'll receive.

The same holds true for e-mail. When everybody has e-mail and anybody can send e-mail, how do you make sure that yours are the messages that are going to be read and responded to first? The answer is—**Brand You.**

From my experience and viewpoint, nobody understands branding better than consulting firms, with their model of the rules of branding embedded at both the firm and individual contributor level.

Almost every consulting firm works with the same business model. They have no hard assets. Just soft assets—people—smart, motivated, talented people. And they have massive revenues and profits.

These firms have an unambiguous culture of work and life. As soon as new recruits start work there, they immediately have to figure out how to deliver value to clients. It's "up or out," "deliver or die."

Along the way, they will learn loads of interesting things, hone their skills, and create a network. The really smart operators learn how to stand out from all the other very smart talent they are internally competing with for that Holy Grail of "partner" status. Along the way, the really smart ones work out what it takes to add value, create a personal brand and a personalized strategy to promote it.

What makes **Brand You** any different? You're every bit as much a brand as Apple, Goldman Sachs, Nike, Coke or Starbucks. So ask yourself . . .

What is it that my product or service does that's special, that makes it uniquely different?

Give yourself the time-honored 20-words-or-less "elevator pitch" challenge. Take the time to write down your answer. And then take the time to read it. Many tImes over.

If your answer wouldn't fire up a prospective client, or command a testimonial from a satisfied former client, or—worst of all—if it doesn't inspire you . . . then start again.

Look at the qualities or characteristics that make you distinctive. What do your friends, family, colleagues or customers say are your greatest strengths? (See also BREAKTHROUGH #8—Know Your Self.)

What is the "feature-benefit model" that **Brand You** offers?

Do you deliver your work on time, every time?

Do your customers get legendary service that meets and exceeds their needs?

Do you always deliver within budget and exceed expectations?

Ask yourself:

> **What do I do that adds remarkable, measurable, distinguished, distinctive value?**

Ask yourself:

> **What do I do that I am most proud of?**

Ask yourself:

> **What have I accomplished that I can unabashedly brag about?**

Since you already are a brand, whether you like it or not, you may as well make it a positive and profitable one. First, identify and relentlessly focus on what it is you do that adds value, that you're proud of, and, most important, that you can shamelessly take credit for.

After you've done that, sit down and ask yourself one more question to define your brand:

What do I want to be famous for?

That's right—famous for!

What's the pitch for **Brand You?**

Don't sell the sausage, sell the sizzle.

- What are your USPs (Unique Selling Points)?
- Your SUPERtalents?
- Your SUPERstrengths?

It's essential to get people singing your praises, because when they do, they'll spread the word about what a remarkable brand you are.

There's no end of ideas for ways you can go about enhancing your profile and marketing your brand, if you put your mind to it.

Get credit for being an expert in something unique. People will come back to you with more opportunities to work together if you stand out from the crowd. Especially if you are not only the best version of yourself but, in being so, you end up as the best at your craft—that is always the best positioning.

Become . . . the Luxury Brand in "X," the Rolls Royce of "Y," the World's Top "Z."

The more often you are seen in the right places and in the right ways by the right people, the more in demand you will be. The hardest part, like most things, is getting started. Write articles. Give presentations. Network.

The next important thing to remember about your personal visibility campaign is that **it all matters.**

When you're promoting **Brand You**, everything you do, and fail to do, communicates the value and character of your brand.

Let's be clear on that old "form over substance" debate. It's both. It's *and*, not *or*. It's absolutely both a matter of substance—what you have to say—AND a matter of style. In a crowded world, packaging counts just as much as content.

Word-of-mouth marketing is critical to any personal branding campaign. Your network of friends, colleagues, clients and customers is the most important marketing vehicle you will ever have. What they say about you and your value-add is what others will relate to initially as the value of your brand. So how can you find ways to nurture your network and get them to talk about **Brand You?**

Remember that we judge people by the company they keep. So, if you want to be seen as the "go-to-person" in your chosen specialty, then make sure that the people you are associated with will be great brand ambassadors for **Brand You**—that they are people you would happily pay to go out and talk about **Brand You** because you know they say great things about you.

So few of my clients initially understand the power of their own **Brand You** or the power of their network, and this is something I work on with them intensively.

Who is in your network?

I have a simple formula when it comes to nurturing my network. I believe that currently there are at least 1,000 people who reciprocally want to know me. In other words, I want to know and have access to them—and they also want to know and have access to me. I have these people in a database and connect with them regularly. I also manage my network proactively by regularly filtering out connections that no longer fit my needs and refreshing the pond with new stock.

For a contact to "fit" my networking strategy:

- I have to like the person
- I have to admire and trust and respect the person
- I have to be willing to refer friends and clients to the person
- I have to feel that the person is to his or her "craft" what I am to mine

And on the basis that someone checks off all of these boxes, my mindset toward that person is always, "What can I do for you?"

I connect people. I send them articles and ideas. I refer to them any people, books, networking opportunities and events that I know they have an interest in. This generosity is central to Brand Me! And I trust that the law of karma/attraction generates flow back to me, directly and indirectly—which it always does.

What's the true POWER of **Brand You?**

By power, I mean influence. Reputational power.

Getting and using your influence—smartly, responsibly, consciously and, yes, powerfully—are essential skills for growing your brand. One of the things that attracts us to brands is the power they project, which is largely a matter of perception.

If you want people to see you as a powerful brand, act like one!

The baby-boomer generation had "jobs for life." Well, no longer! An old-fashioned résumé won't get you anywhere anymore! You need a marketing piece and pitch for **Brand You.** Instead of a list of job titles and dates, your brand marketing bio should bring to life the skills you've mastered, the projects you've delivered, the achievements that you can take credit for.

Instead of a life as a slave on the corporate career ladder, you need to reinvent yourself using the modern work paradigm of "projects."

Start by writing your own VISION Statement and MISSION Statement. What turns you on? Is it . . .

> **Recognition:** for your skills as a guru?

> **Nurturing:** do you take new business ideas from concept to market?

> **Talent:** can you express your unique gift?

Success: what's your personal definition of success? Money . . . Power . . . Fame? Or doing what you love?

However you answer these questions, search relentlessly for project opportunities that will deliver your Vision and allow you to express your Mission. And review those Vision and Mission Statements regularly to make sure you still believe and resonate with what you wrote.

Being CEO of **Brand You** requires you to promote yourself. However, never let hubris get in the way. Remember always to . . .

Be authentic and be a "people person."

Be the best at something that adds real value—and has real outcomes . . . and

Be a visionary.

It's that simple.

You may want to get a mentor to act as your sounding board. (See BREAKTHROUGH #20.) It's good to be held accountable by someone independent, who has no conflict of interest, no ax to grind, no hidden agenda, nor any vested interest in the outcome—other than your success.

Even though I mentor others, I always have a mentor (or two) to whom I can download and from whom I receive new insights and get a sense-check on things. And it's surprising how often they serve to remind me, "I thought you'd planned to do X, not Y?"—rather than what I was actually doing.

I often have a perfectly valid reason for the change that I haven't filled them in on—but it's always good to keep a check on my thinking to ensure that it is aligned with Brand Me by justifying it to an experienced and detached mentor.

When you do the right things the right way (BREAKTHROUGH #6) and you follow your own personal North Star (BREAKTHROUGH #1) you are on the path to creating a **Brand You** that others will want to connect with, both personally and professionally.

Breakthrough #8

Know Your Self

To be truly "great," a leader needs to be highly self-aware. This is different to "knowledge."

New forms of technology and communication, and ever-expanding volumes of knowledge, mean that less than 10 percent of the information we need to operate In life can be successfully contained in our brains. Compare this figure to 75 percent, just 20 years ago.

Hence the old mantra that "knowledge is power" is no longer valid, and our genetic default program no longer works or applies.

Being self-aware–rather than simply possessing "knowledge"–is the new key to power. True power involves earning the trust, respect and loyalty of the people we engage with in life. As leaders, if we wish to inspire such qualities, along with continuous learning and engagement in others, this shift first needs to start within ourselves.

Self-awareness is also a prerequisite if you want to achieve personal BREAKTHROUGHs.

How self-aware are you?

Do you know your personality type and style?

Do you THINK your way to solutions—or FEEL your way? Do you like to leave things open or make judgments and decisions quickly? Do you think rationally when making decisions—or intuitively—or both?

How do you best LEARN—through reading, just doing, planning, or by exploring options?

Which SENSES are your most dominant—seeing, hearing, touch, listening?

Are you competitive? Are you optimistic? Do you like change? Which emotions are most likely to trigger you? (More on this in BREAKTHROUGH #16.)

What are your values? Do you have a sense of ethics?

Self-awareness is about what makes us tick. It extends beyond finding our North Star (see BREAKTHROUGH #1), and understanding our emotions and beliefs (remember BREAKTHROUGH #2?), to what drives and motivates us. It involves having an awareness of our deep "drivers"—which includes our VALUES.

A value is simply something that we hold dear. Something we place importance on that gives meaning and purpose to our lives.

Our values are like the navigation system that guides us—and our sense of ethics and morality. They guide us to be the very best version of ourselves—and to our eventual Destiny.

Without having clarity about what our values are, we are sailing blind.

There are two types of values—ENDS Values and MEANS Values.

Means Values are connected to our emotional needs–for example, "money."

An Ends Value is "love," i.e., the emotional state I desire.

"Family" would be a Means Value when it's a means to the Ends Values of LOVE, SECURITY, or HAPPINESS.

Too many people pursue Means Values oblivious to the Ends Values that they truly desire. And eventually, despite having "made their fortune" or "gotten the girl" or "built their empire," there is a sad hollowness to their victory that they are puzzled by until they realize that their true objective was love or happiness.

You'll know you are chasing Means Values anytime you find yourself questioning, "Is this it? Is this what's at the end of the rainbow?"

Well, no, Einstein, it's not!

Seek Ends Values like love, freedom, intimacy, health, passion, adventure–and you will find them–and also the path to happiness.

Equally, too many people are concerned with their reputation, rather than their character.

Our character is who we really are, whereas our reputation is who others think we are.

Achieving clarity around my own values has helped me understand why I do what I do and why I do it in the way I do.

We have "nature" values and "nurture" values–and they sometimes conflict. There were times as a child when my mom would want me to do South, but my heart felt like doing North, and I would feel a tug between those two polarities. So knowing what my own "nature" values are, as well as those I have learned and decided to embrace as my own (my "nurture" values), helps me make better and smarter decisions.

I have noticed a simple binary rule. When I live in accordance with my "nurture" values and my highest standards, I feel complete joy. And when I don't, it always goes wrong!

This is why I work hard to understand the values and character of my clients and the key people in my life.

If ever we are unclear about which choice to make, or things are going wrong, it's nearly always due to lack of clarity about our true values.

Ask yourself what values you need in order to achieve your dreams, to be the very best version of yourself and to achieve your ultimate Destiny.

Explore and embrace as your birthright values like vitality and health, love and warmth, creativity, making a difference, a passion for growth and learning, curiosity, fun and happiness, passion and honesty, boldness and adventure—and accept that these are who you truly are. Then settle for nothing less.

When you commit and hold yourself accountable to these values as a way of life, you show up as the very best version of yourself.

Here is the Top 10 list of values—or, as some might call them, virtues—that I believe serve everyone universally. These are present in all the great leaders I have worked with.

1. Fairness

2. Truth and honesty

3. Trustworthiness

4. Excellence

5. Conscientiousness

6. Integrity

7. Humility

8. Forgiveness

9. Patience

10. Altruistic love

How do you rate your score out of ten in each of these values?

If something is missing in your life, figure out which value you need to add to your list and then incorporate it into your daily life. Practice until perfect. And any values that don't serve you ("nurture" values) should be ditched—or refined. When the values that support your "dream" life are alive and vibrant inside you—they will begin to be alive and vibrant in all that surrounds you.

Most people think they know themselves better than anyone else does. But the reality is that others see in us that which we cannot see in ourselves—our strengths, vulnerabilities and our future potential. We each have attributes that come so easily to us that we aren't even able to identify or name them (i.e., areas of strength in which we are "unconsciously competent").

We also have blind spots (i.e., "unconscious incompetencies") about what we could be doing differently that would maximize our abilities or capabilities.

The importance of obtaining feedback from the people who know us best cannot be overemphasized. The best way I've found to do this with my clients is using a values-based feedback tool that I facilitate with my business partner, Joan.

Identifying Values

The Leadership Values Assessment (LVA) is a 360 degree (360°) feedback instrument that invites the person being assessed and their assessors to give input on the subject's:

- operating values
- strengths or positive attributes
- issues that, if addressed, will unleash the leader's potential
- general feedback.

Here's what my own LVA looks like . . .

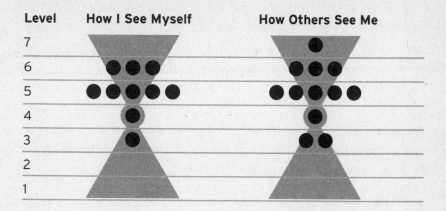

Value (How I See Myself)	Level	Value (How Others See Me) from my 27 Assessors	No. out of 27	Level
commitment	5	commitment	11	5
generosity	5	generosity	10	5
positive attitude	5	positive attitude	10	5
making a difference	6	making a difference	8	6
results orientation	3	results orientation	8	3
intuition	6	intuition	7	6
personal development	4	continuous learning	11	4
inspiration	5	vision	10	7
balance (physical/emotional/ mental/spiritual)	6	integrity	7	5
humor/fun	5	honesty	7	5
		ambition	9	3
		leadership development	7	6

Exact matching values   Similar matching values

This instrument is based on the premise that there is no "right" formula or set of competencies that make a person successful, and that in fact great leaders come in all shapes and sizes and present a variety of styles. It also provides the clarification and understanding of what a leader is doing well; i.e., his or her strengths. It is most effective in moving the person forward rather than focusing on what is "wrong." Being conscious of their values and how they are coming across (or not) is important because of the impact values have on any leader's actions, decisions, culture, and relationships.

How the LVA Works

The first step in this process is the creation of the survey, which is customized for each leader in respect of the list of values from which to select. The survey is then put online and comes with a unique user name and password for the leader and for the assessors. The leader completes the survey for him or herself and then sends the codes to the 15–30 people who know the leader best, professionally and personally. The assessors are given the choice to enter their names or complete the online survey anonymously.

Regular updates are sent to the leader, reporting how many people have completed the survey to date. Once it is closed, the data is downloaded, plotted, and analyzed in a written report. The feedback on "Strengths" and "Areas of Improvement" is collated, themed, and listed in the report.

In the end, two reports comprise the LVA—one being the "dot plot" diagram that visually compares the alignment of the leader's values to those perceived by his or her assessors and how they fall onto the

Seven Levels of Consciousness in Leadership model that underpins the LVA.

The second part of the report is the analysis of the values data, including the list of Strengths, Areas of Improvement, and Feedback.

Once the report has been written, it's time to go through the results with the leader. This is done in a one-to-one session with Joan that takes around two hours (I guess I should say two-on-one, as I always sit in and become involved when I do this with clients as part of their retreat).

The debrief with Joan opens with the following questions:

Briefly describe who you are—your work, position, professional and personal interests.

- What is your 360° assessment experience?
- What are your strengths?
- What would your boss say your strengths are?
- What would your wife/husband/life partner say your strengths are?
- What are your children proud of you for?
- What do you want to improve or stop?
- What gets you up in the morning?
- What do you most excel at; i.e., what is the biggest gift you bring to any table you sit at? What is the gift or competence you bring to the group discussion?

- What is the best thing that your assessors could have said about you; i.e., that would touch or please you the most?

- What is the worst or most upsetting thing they could have said about you?

- On a scale of one to ten, what is your willingness to stop or change a behavior?

The answers to these questions provide insight into what matters to this particular leader, their level of self-awareness, and their openness to the feedback data.

Why the LVA Works

For many, this is their first 360 degree (360°) assessment, the first time they have had one in their current position, or the first time they have had one in a number of years. Whatever the case, as humans we are naturally interested in what other people think of us or believe about us.

Almost always (if not always) leaders are surprised by the richness of the data, the positive or affirming nature of the input and the accuracy of what people are seeing. The data is rarely, if ever, as negative as the leader fears it is going to be. In fact, the opposite occurs. The input from the assessors does the following:

- Eliminates possible doubts that the leader has about what people are thinking or perceiving

- Increases self-confidence regarding the leader's contributions, strengths and abilities

- Expands the leader's awareness of what he or she brings to the table, including what the leader is good at and to what degree, what the leader is good at and didn't know, and how behaviors are being interpreted

- Outlines what distinguishes this person from other leaders and informs him or her how to capitalize on these assets

- Names the "elephants in the room," with suggestions for how to move forward

With all the cards on the table regarding what the leader perceives about his or herself and what the assessors think of the leader, patterns become clear around:

- What is working

- What needs to be activated more

- What needs to change for the leader to reach his or her desired goal/position/state

- The pictures of what is and what could be are on the wall for the leader to take in—and then take action

The sooner we accept how others see us—and our even greater potential—the faster we can step into it completely and be our whole selves, effectively and powerfully. Achieving this next step in our growth and personal evolution leads to the start of a new and even bigger picture.

Some individuals may find it a valuable exercise to contact the company that conducts the LVA, www.valuescentre.com, and arrange for one of their accredited trainers to set up the tool and a debrief.

Alternatively, you can use the simple 360-degree (360°) tool in the BREAKTHROUGH RETREAT WORKBOOK at the end of this book (see TOOL #7).

Either way, understanding what your values are and how they serve you adds to your self-awareness in a way that will help you make much better choices on your way to personal mastery and being the best version of yourself.

You will recognize and experience that making choices in alignment with your values puts you in FLOW and in The Zone—and how the reverse is equally true!

It's not a hard choice to make, is it?

Breakthrough #9

May the Force Be With You

One of my business partners, Joy, is an acupuncturist specializing in Five Elements Theory. She arrives at my client's retreat or mentoring session armed with a box of needles and an approach based on 3,000 years of classical Chinese medicine.

She is about to spend the next three hours exploring our client's most elemental makeup and asking the question, "Where's the loose brick?" Once found, she uses traditional acupuncture to put the errant brick back in place and "make the whole structure stable."

How it Works

If that sounds a bit disrespectful, it's not meant to be. It's just a shorthand way of describing what is at the heart of all of us. For as human beings (even the most extraordinarily successful ones) we all have our weaknesses, vulnerabilities and character traits that predispose us to less-than-perfect performance.

In Chinese medicine, which emphasizes the interconnectedness of mind, body and spirit, those performance hiccups can (and very often do) span physical as well as mental/emotional areas.

They also connect up so that emotional issues will typically emerge in specific and related bodily complaints—and vice versa. For example, the CEO with high blood pressure may very well have corresponding issues with unexpressed anger, while the philanthropist hell-bent on feeding the world might have digestive and metabolic disorders like IBS or diabetes.

On more subtle levels, while the physical body may be kept in good shape (my clients typically place high value on this), underlying emotional imbalances might emerge instead as unhelpful attitudinal and behavioral traits. For example, the corporate warrior might be so "afraid" of losing control that he consistently fails to delegate, or the celebrity, so in need of love, that she plays only to the crowd and never acknowledges an inner sadness.

More rarefied still, the imbalances can manifest in what might be called "spiritual malaise," where the body keeps busy but the person's sense of self is diminished or confused.

These people can appear highly driven and effective on the outside, but carry a deep sense of something missing inside. These are patterns that are often so deeply ingrained that they have become "us." They are the invisible baggage that, if left undetected and untreated throughout a whole life, can weigh us down and block our true potential.

These are the patterns that the acupuncturist works hard to detect. Her questions, tests and observations are designed to assess those hardwired traits that have been there since birth and which are influencing how that person lives life on the physical, emotional and spiritual levels.

Joy draws a diagram that shows how all of the client's issues are linked and, very often, how they can be traced back to an elemental imbalance (her "loose brick" analogy). The acupuncture given during the retreat is designed both to clear any residual blocks to treatment and to start the process of correcting the elemental imbalance. She then leads a short discussion, with the client and with me, the mentor, in which she explains how the imbalance is manifesting and what the implications might be.

Why it Works

Chinese Five Elements Theory perceives that all of Nature—ourselves included—is made up of the five Elements: Fire, Earth, Metal, Water and Wood. These Elements all influence one another and exist in a unique "cocktail combination" in each of us—a kind of "energetic DNA."

Our unique elemental makeup will dictate how we interact with the world—making us who we are. In perfect health, these Elements are well balanced and harmonious. In ill health, they are out of balance and distorted. Each Element expresses itself in our emotions, our appearance—even in the sound of our voice and in our body odor. When one Element needs more support than the others or when one is dominating the scene, it will show up in our attitudes and emotional responses, as well as in health issues such as those already described.

So, when Joy examines a new client, she is looking for the clues that will reveal which Element is "running the show." When she finds this, she is going to the very heart of a person's issues—the thing that has been predisposing this person toward recurring unhelpful behaviors or that has been showing up for years as a chronic bad back!

The Consultation

For many people, this will be the first time that their medical history, lifestyle, emotions, attitudes and behaviors have been explored and linked together. This consultation process alone can be a powerful and liberating experience, with clients being guided through old emotional patterns in the safe and confidential space of a retreat.

The Diagnosis

By producing a diagram, which shows how all of the client's health issues (physical, emotional, spiritual) are linked, Joy cuts through what can seem to be the confused picture of a person's life issues with clarity and simplicity. This gives a strong sense of control back to the client. The client sees clearly that if he or she can just deal with the core issue, all of the others will get better.

The Treatment

The acupuncture treatment during the retreat does several things. First, it is designed to clear any blocks to treatment, which might have built up over the subject's life. In a very simple treatment involving acupuncture on the back, Joy draws out what she calls "aggressive energy"—a kind of energetic sludge that can accumulate in the channels as a result of demanding lifestyles. That done, she then chooses points that are specific to the subject's particular elemental imbalance and delivers a treatment designed to strengthen or correct any deficiency.

Most people come out of this session feeling deeply relaxed and content, and start to glimpse how acupuncture treatment can help them move forward.

The Discussion

The final discussion, in which insights are shared and the implications of the diagnosis are explored, can be a profound experience in which clients acknowledge, often for the first time, where their issues are rooted. They leave this session with a clear sense of what needs to be addressed and how their life will improve when that is done.

Most important, their energy has been shifted to "open them up" to the mentoring and BREAKTHROUGHs that are to follow.

Breakthrough #10

From WillPower and WayPower . . . to WavePower

Once we have new levels of clarity around your values and how you are perceived by others from your LVA assessment, and have begun to address your Five Element constitutional patterns . . . what then?

It's time for the *Breakingthrough* session . . . with my business partner, Jennifer Moalem.

This next step involves going even deeper in terms of identifying outdated patterns comprising beliefs, attitudes, values and behaviors—and then breaking through them.

There's much more involved in creating genuine and lasting transformation than just acquiring knowledge about the patterns you need to change—or even having sufficient **WillPower**—to follow through with actions based on that knowledge.

Within the retreat environment, isolated from outside influences, it's easy to commit to letting go of patterns we've identified as limiting, and to having the courage to act from newly identified strengths.

However, stepping back into the "everyday" world, the forces exerted on you by the various influences vested in maintaining the status quo—from family to business partners—can be overwhelmingly powerful.

Despite your best efforts, even with unlimited **WayPower** (or resources), it's easy to slide back into old patterns and even sabotage your new intentions. That is, unless we also shift you out of "resonance" with your old patterns and into alignment with the new.

Without the coherence or **WavePower** that comes from being fully aligned with, or "resonating" with, being the best version of yourself—as well as your intentions and new possibilities—you will either not achieve them, or you will expend far more energy and resources than necessary in doing so.

Our "Secret Weapon"

My business partner, Jennifer, brings to the mentoring journey more than 25 years of exploration and pioneering in the field of human potential and Energy Psychology. She begins preparing our clients in the weeks leading up to the retreat by asking them the questions:

> What is the BREAKTHROUGH that you currently don't think or believe is possible?. . .

> The BREAKTHROUGH that would give you the edge? . . .

A BREAKTHROUGH that might also inspire others to change or transform in some way?

Often, clients struggle to come up with answers—or will respond with a list of business and personal "goals."

During their first day of the retreat, clues begin to emerge about what the real BREAKTHROUGH might be for them. They understand that specific shifts may be required in terms of their values and their patterns of thinking and behavior. They begin to see aspects of themselves that they were not aware of, or were perhaps previously unable to articulate.

The results of Joan's Leadership Values Assessment and a summary of Joy's insights into constitutional patterns, along with any additional feedback or recommendations from me, are forwarded to Jennifer prior to the client's final intervention during the retreat. She then compiles this data in a way that allows her to laser in on what's relevant during the *Breakingthrough* session.

Drawing on a potent cocktail of principles from Quantum Physics, New Biology, psychology, ancient wisdom and systems of healing (i.e., Chinese Five Elements, chakras, and more)—and, for added efficacy, some kinesiology—she uses tools that "cut to the chase," to effectively realign the client with his or her potential in a life-altering way.

This session supports the client in integrating all that has unfolded during the course of the retreat, and clears the way for them to experience ongoing and, more important, sustainable, positive change.

By the end of the *Breakingthrough* session with Jennifer, our clients have begun actually to embody being the "best version of themselves."

Even the most resistant will say things like, "I was really skeptical, but I just feel different." Those who dare to engage more deeply will often report back with comments like, "This session changed my life!"

Tracking Your WavePower

Every session is completely different because it's determined by what the client's system needs for the particular issues that we've identified based on the results of the LVA, the feedback from the Five Elements assessment—and what the client's system is ready for as their "next step."

The tool of kinesiology, or muscle checking, is used during the *Breakingthrough* session to track information about the client's autonomic nervous system and any patterns that enhance or deplete their energy. This scientifically validated method of obtaining a simple "yes" or "no" biofeedback response has its origins in chiropractic.

Throughout each session, Jennifer is continually checking for resonance (or "wave frequency") and identifying any subtle energy imbalances in the field. She is not identifying or diagnosing actual symptoms or issues, or attempting to "fix" a problem.

However, when your resonance shifts, what you experience as "reality" can change—and that change can manifest in any of the six spokes in your Wheel of Life.

Put simply . . .

WavePower amplifies your WillPower and your WayPower!

Working with Jennifer is about moving you out of resonance with what you don't want—and into resonance or alignment with who you do want to BE, and with what you want to DO and HAVE.

How WavePower Works

Science tells us that everything is made up of energy that pulsates at different rates and frequencies. Modern technology allows us to perceive clearly, as a fact, that information is transmitted as wave frequency or vibration (e.g., in cell phones, TV, remote controls, etc.).

However, most people don't extend that understanding to their physical body, their thoughts and emotions—or to events they experience in life.

In the physical body, all of our organs and glands have a frequency or resonance—in fact, that's what MRI (Magnetic Resonance Imaging) machines "read" when they scan us. Any pain or symptom that we experience in our body is also a vibrational frequency that is resonating outside of the "healthy" or normal range.

Similarly, all of our emotions can also be measured as frequency. Most people can "feel the vibe" in the presence of a partner, boss or colleague who is stressed, or in a bad mood. And we might also be aware of how our own bad moods can magnetize or trigger the same in others, or attract a cascade of less than optimal events!

Linking these observations, we recognize that all of our problems or challenges are also "frequencies"—somewhat like being stuck on a radio station we don't like.

Equally, our goals, visions, and dreams–and also that "best version" of ourselves that we are seeking–are like the radio station we want to be tuned into. However, instead of clear reception, we're getting "static."

Utilizing WavePower means understanding that what we, as human beings, are "tuned in" to, or resonate with, is what we will experience in life.

Are we M : A : D?

In ways that complement the LVA and Five Elements analysis, each *Breakingthrough* session also illuminates where you may think you're resonating with certain values, but not living in alignment with them.

Jennifer identifies where you are resonating with beliefs, attitudes, difficult past experiences, and even generational or cultural patterns, that serve to block you from living "in tune" with your full potential. For example, if you resonate with the frequency of values like honesty or transparency, then that tends to be what you'll express–and attract– in business and in life. However, if you resonate with the frequencies of anger, control and conflict, then you'll either express anger, be controlling, or tend to attract angry, controlling people who generate conflict around you–or both.

We can also resonate with a person–or with their thoughts, ideas, creativity, or vision. We might affectionately refer to the "mad" inventor, or people's "mad" ideas or visions. But what's the difference between a person, vision, idea, or project being "mad" in the sense of a little crazy–and those that are M : A : D in the way we'd prefer–that is, "Making A Difference"?

Throughout history there have been pioneers, explorers, musicians, artists, and visionaries—from leaders like Gandhi and Nelson Mandela, to great composers and inventors—whose vision or creativity is literally a "wave" of energy that others identify with and are inspired by. Long after the passing of the individual, the legacy—from the works of Michelangelo, to Beethoven's symphonies, or the poetry of Rumi—can still "move" us because of its resonance . . . this is WavePower in action.

How do we know when we are not in tune with our own highest values and potential? Clues arrive when we want to achieve something—we think we are aligned with it, and yet there seem to be endless obstacles and challenges. We'll experience roadblocks, achieve what we want and be unable to sustain it, or else something happens and we lose it. Often this occurs because of deeply held, sometimes unwitting beliefs, many of which arise from our earlier experiences.

. . . only a B : I : T ?

What is it then that "makes the difference"—that inspires greatness in oneself and in others?

It's simply "Being In Tune"—firstly with self-awareness, and then integrating that self-awareness—to live as the optimal version of Self.

It's only when we relate with others, and the World, from that place of centeredness and coherence that we can unfold and be in alignment with expressing our true contribution and Legacy.

Unless we are "relational"—not just with people, but we embrace our interconnectedness and relationality with everything in the Universe—we will want to "change the World" from a place of ego.

When we resonate with truly "being of service," changing ourselves changes the World.

Like the Marianne Williamson quote in my Introduction says, ". . . **as we let our own light shine, we unconsciously give other people permission to do the same."**

When we are living as Beings In Tune (B : I : Ts), contributing our unique "bit," and also allowing others to do the same, somehow all the B : I : Ts fit together harmoniously.

. . . and are you really B : O : S?

This final session in our retreat is about closing the gap between where you are and not just where you would prefer to be, but who you truly are. It's about shifting into greater alignment with your true and optimal potential, with that best version of your Self—and also having the humility to realize that "best" is an ongoing and inner personal journey rather than some long-coveted "destination"!

Your tomorrow is determined by what you resonate with today—and each new day attracts opportunities according to your resonance.

Continuing to fine-tune and hone your resonance is fundamental to achieving the kind of lasting positive change that allows you to make a *real* difference—and leave a M : A : D Legacy that is truly "Being Of Service" (B : O : S).

Adding WavePower to this proven combination of BREAKTHROUGH "power tools" and the mentoring process supports you to become the best possible B : O : S—a leader in your field, and in life!

Breakthrough #11

Love Is a Verb

Of all of the many areas in our lives where we can achieve BREAKTHROUGHs, from health to wealth and lasting happiness, the one area that preoccupies most people much of the time is the area of love.

Relationships are amongst the most important experiences of our lives. Everything we understand and experience about ourselves we can only ever do in the context of our relationships with others.

That is why we yearn for meaningful relationships. That's why the lack of conscious relationships in our lives causes most of us pain and suffering. The thing that's supposed to bring us the greatest joy often brings us the greatest pain.

So, why is that? What's going on? Well, here is what I've figured out.

Most of us get into relationships for the wrong reasons. Not for reasons that have anything to do with our North Star and overall Life's Purpose.

A joyful relationship is not an oxymoron. I now believe that . . .

Only if my reason for entering into a new relationship is aligned to my soul's reason for being, can that relationship ever be sacred and joyful.

Until a few years ago, when I had a major BREAKTHROUGH about love, I believed that I wasn't lovable.

I want and have always wanted three things:

- I want to be loved
- I want affection
- I want appreciation

Because I believed that I was not lovable, I accepted relationships in which I wasn't loved, or where there was no affection or appreciation.

And now, as a result of this BREAKTHROUGH, I believe and know I am indeed lovable.

Just as I have always done, I continue to:

- Love others
- Appreciate others
- Be affectionate to others

. . . but now without needing them to reciprocate!

And all of the love and affection and appreciation that I now enjoy comes to me from so many people, in so many wonderful ways.

In the past, I began relationships with one eye looking at what I hoped I could get out of them. Not in a cruel or premeditated or selfish way— but rather in a naïve and ignorant way. I noticed that when I stopped getting out of the relationship what I'd hoped to get out of it, I wanted to get out of the relationship, too—and so did the other person!

Although a serial monogamist, I went through relationship after relationship, looking for that perfect mate who could finally complete me and make me whole.

Surely there was someone out there who could see me for who I truly was—and share with me that eternal happiness I was sure we both wanted? Especially when I was willing to do "my bit and more" in barter!

I even thought, somewhat arrogantly, that I could figure out what the other person wanted—and that I would then provide it for them. I also learned to hide certain traits of my own that I had realized were not, perhaps, attractive to others.

Toward the end of a few relationships that I was trying to keep alive, I ended up loathing myself for the pretzel-shaped contortions that I would put myself into to keep a dysfunctional relationship going. It was as if I was saying, "What other part of me should I set aside or twist in order to keep us together?"

It was painful holding back on saying what I wanted to say, thinking what I truly thought and doing what I truly wanted to do. It was painful holding in WHO I TRULY AM.

I realized I was bartering for a relationship. *You give me this and I'll give you that.* And when the bartering stopped, so did the relationship.

I was fed up with being fed up. It was time to understand the problem, break the pattern and reach a solution.

And what I learned was the most beautiful and simple thing.

What I learned is that **the purpose of a relationship has nothing to do with what I can get out of it and everything to do with what I put into it.**

Not putting something in as a trade for what I could get out; rather, putting something in as a means of understanding myself and who I truly am.

If the real me isn't sufficient to keep the other person interested in being in a relationship with me, I now accept, quite happily, that it's time to move on.

Never again will I deny the real me. I will always be authentic in what I put into a relationship from here on.

Only by being authentic, can I attract someone who genuinely likes me for who I truly am. And when they do show up, they will want to stay with me in response to my authenticity. The tap dance is forever over.

I now understand how relationships help me to define myself—to know my Self better. With the right person, I get to know and be my authentic Self. In the context of such a magical relationship, I resonate with and can be the very best version of myself—and so can my partner.

I now understand that I can only know and see in myself what I know and see in others. I can only like or dislike in them what I like and dislike in myself. And to the extent that I fail to recognize the GRACE in others, I cannot know it in myself.

And so what I have learned is that the primary purpose of any relationship is for me to see the highest potential, the North Star, the grandest vision of the other, and then to assist that person in creating it.

I believe it was the Buddha who said:

"Love is the selfless promotion of the growth of the other."

So a relationship is what I can do for you. It's about what I give to you.

It's about how I help you become the very best version of yourself.

It's not about what I get or what you can do for me.

And what's in all of this selflessness for me?

Well, I get to be the very best version of myself.

And attract others, like you, who also choose to be the best version of Self. In the famous refrain from The Beatles song, "Love is all you need."

Love in Action!

When a client says to me, "David, I am struggling in my relationship with my partner. I'm not in love anymore. What should I do?" my answer is simple. "Go and love him."

The client then might say, "Perhaps you didn't hear me. I said I'm not in love with my partner anymore. What should I do now?" I say, "Love him. Go and love him. Go and do things that will help your partner, and expect nothing in return. Help your partner become the very best version of Self."

When we experience a relationship in this way, we transform our whole experience of OURSELVES with our loved ones. As a result, we neither want nor expect anything from them—and just want to give to them. And we seek to give them everything we can, needing nothing in return, because this is us, working at our highest potential.

But let's be clear. This isn't an invitation to them to take advantage of us. Or abuse our generosity. This isn't an excuse for us to be a saintly victim in a dysfunctional heist. No! We also have to love ourselves. Which is why we have to move on if we are being abused or if we are not being loved in return.

I know my former wife thought it was rather strange at the time, but after a year of working unbelievably hard to resuscitate my last marriage, I chose to close that chapter of my life, even though I still loved her. I chose to love her *and* help her have what she wanted in life—which she couldn't find with me—and I chose to love *and* accept that my needs for love, affection and appreciation were not being met by her and never would be. I felt empowered to say to her, "I love you *and* choose to divorce you," and not to see these parts of the same sentence as being in conflict with each other.

I accepted that our time as a couple was over. It was time for us to love each other (and our children) on separate life paths. Just because certain critical-to-me behaviors were not in alignment with how I wanted to live my life didn't mean I didn't love her. And still do. And always will.

Today we are friends and speak the truth to each other openly, without any need to find fault with what was.

Although not the biological mother of my children, she is their spiritual mother, and we continue to share our joint love for them as earnestly as we did when we were a couple.

The best way for a relationship to thrive is for there to be no conditions. No limitations. Such a relationship is based on true love and on freedom, which is the essence of love.

FREEDOM is the essence of WHO WE ARE. If we love someone, we will never seek to restrict him or her in any way. Love says, "I choose for you what you choose for you," otherwise known as THE PLATINUM RULE. (See BREAKTHROUGH #12.)

And here is the ultimate irony of this way of thinking. The moment we say, "I choose for you what you choose for yourself," your partner will never leave because we all really want to be with someone who will give us what we want.

We want our partner to say to us:

"I recognize that you will change. Your ideas will change, your tastes will change, and your dreams and desires will change. And as that happens you will even change your own understanding of who you are and what's important for you. I want you to be the very best version of yourself—full stop."

. . . and if we receive that, then why would such a relationship ever end?

There should only ever be one requirement of each other— AUTHENTICITY. Be the best version of yourself. And if you love me for anything, love me because I live my life the same way.

What could ever be more delicious than being told:

"I love you the most when you are exactly the way you are right now."

"What? Even though I'm a bit overweight and am obsessive-compulsive and all those other faults you tease me about?"

"I not only love you in spite of those things, I love you because of them."

That's love. Everything else is counterfeit.

Finding fault in yourself or others is about our fears—and FEAR is nothing more than . . .

False

Evidence

Appearing

Real

Your "faults" in one person's eyes are your "gifts" in another's. The *right* other. And sometimes it's not that these faults are deal-breakers, it's just that the dial level is set too high or too low. Turn the dial up or down and see how quickly the other person's reactions change.

Great relationships are grounded in solid foundations, where we choose to see in the other what we choose to see in ourselves. Where we give to the other what we choose to receive. Where what we take from the other, we take from ourselves. And how do we do that?

With three magic words: **AS YOU WISH.**

The issues in most relationships boil down to sex and money.

And within that, the time, the availability and the activities of the other. People crave quality time and shared experiences. The simple truth is that people in a relationship want the other person's attention and time. It's a power struggle.

In a great relationship, there are no power struggles. In a non-threatening way, one person would simply say to the other:

"You must do as you wish, but I need to share with you that what you are doing doesn't feel good for me. It's okay if you want to do it. However, if this is something you wish to continue, then I may need to move on."

There is no threat involved. It's simply a communication about what works for the individual.

It's saying:

"You know, I really do want to share my life with a beloved other and I would love it if you chose to be that beloved other. And it's also okay if you choose to do something other than what I'd prefer. I won't resent you or be angry or upset—I want you to do what you want to do. You aren't wrong in wanting to do it. You must do AS YOU WISH. I'm just sharing with you what doesn't work for me. My first choice is that I am in a relationship with you, and I also have other options and choices—just as you do. And so, by sharing this, we can both make informed choices!"

Love never struggles with power. Never!

And as a result of giving up that power struggle, we gain something we never dreamed possible. We begin to like ourselves. We begin to love ourselves, appreciate ourselves, and even be affectionate with ourselves.

I know that others could view this as somewhat narcissistic, but for the first time in my life I now like my appearance. I like my attitudes and ideas and beliefs and life goals and values and outlook and worldview. Do you like yours?

I like my wackiness and my spontaneity. And as I love those things in me, I seem to see only those things in the people around me.

I love the company of the friends in my circle now. I like our shared energy.

I no longer feel that anything is missing. Feeling whole no longer depends on one person filling the role of "partner" or "wife."

Here is a poem I wrote at the time I had this BREAKTHROUGH:

No More Empty Chairs

One day, you finally wake up and realize
that there is no one missing from that empty
chair facing you at life's "table for one."

It's been strangely lonely sitting there for a while,
alone, with no one to share each meal and night with.
Uncomfortable, waiting for someone to show up and
quietly sit down and join you and turn those gazing
eyes on to their next people-watching target.

And then you realize. The person missing was no one else.

It was you.

Nervous yet excitedly, shyly yet flirtatiously, you invite
yourself to join you. You chat, you smile, you wonder.
You dream, you cry, you laugh out loud. And at the end

of the date, you know for sure that you enjoyed the time
together and you definitely want to meet up again.

Quickly, it seems, a new and important romance erupts
and you can't get this new friend out of your mind
and can't wait to see them and spend time with them
again. You hope they call and you want to call them.

You think of small gifts that you hope might please
them—knowing that it's the thought that they will
appreciate as much as the gift itself. And of course you
realize that your greatest gift to them is your love.

You welcome them and embrace them into your life and
you nurture this newfound friendship and hope that it
will blossom in time into the special look and feel that
you have seen in others, and that you have admired
and gazed on with a knowing fondness and wonder.

Then . . . and only then, when there are no more
empty chairs, is it time to invite someone to join
your table and drink with you the wine of your
life and share with you the food of your soul.

Many friends grace my table now, as self-love brings with it a
tremendous love for other people.

I have one friend I go to the movies with, another to the opera with,
another to stay up with until 3:00 a.m. debating the meaning of existence,

another who mentors me, and others who play different roles in my life. I have serious friends and fun friends. And every one of them I love. I love them unconditionally and want to help them become the best versions of themselves—and I accept their reciprocal gift of wanting the same for me.

I am attracted to a monogamous "beloved other" relationship when I meet a special someone who sees me as I see myself and who sees me as I imagine myself to be—as the very best version of myself—and who loves me unconditionally and helps me be WHO I TRULY AM.

That special someone sees me the way I see myself and also sees beyond what I can see—sees more than I see in myself. I "settle" for nothing less.

That special someone sees and affirms my most daring and bold thoughts about my potential. I do the same for that person.

When you are with the right person, he or she says those only-imaginable-by-yourself things, like:

> "I have never known anyone so generous or kind or thoughtful as you."

> "You are an amazing and gentle and generous and thoughtful lover."

> "You are making a difference in the world."

> "You are wise."

> "You are eccentric in a charming and delightful way."

And you will do the same thing for this person, reflecting back the things that affirm all of his or her imagined and actual potential.

Love is a verb—love is a choice—love is a decision.

And I know that when I live this way, by changing my behaviors and my beliefs about LOVE, it is attracted into my life in the EXACT way I magnetize it.

I am always mindful about what I want to attract. A conversation with an old Indian gentleman, who was married to his 11-year-old bride when he was himself only 14, was a turning point for me.

He told me how for the first ten years that they were together, they both spent all of their time learning "how to love each other." Learning what the other needed to be the best version of themself. Then they spent the next 50 years working at their marriage and their family. He emphasized that it was loving and fun and all he wanted, but he also emphasized that he only ever got out what he put in. He told me that for the last ten years (they had been married for 70!) he'd been truly "in love." He was living inside love. In a life full of love. I thought that was very beautiful. His advice to me was to be sure what being "in love" would look like to me and to stay conscious of it—and in that way I would attract it to me.

So after several weeks of really thinking through consciously, for the first time in my life, what I truly deeply wanted, this is what I came up with.

1. INTIMACY
2. RESPECT
3. TRUST
4. COMMITMENT
5. COMMUNICATIONS
6. MUTUALITY
7. VERBAL AFFECTION
8. PHYSICAL AFFECTON
9. LOVE
10. FUN

The ending of a relationship that doesn't allow you to be the best version of yourself isn't a tragedy. The tragedy would be staying in it. Or in doing nothing to try and change it into something that would work better for both of you.

The Universe works in extraordinary ways. When I stop trying to understand it or judge it and just allow (rather than resist) what's happening, then and only then do I find the peace and joy that lives inside me. It's in me. Not in someone else. Not out there.

So when I stop looking out there for the one who will make me whole, then and only then do I have the peace and joy and happiness that I seek. I have found it in the place it always was, and that's inside me.

My greatest joy and GRACE is when I selflessly help another to become the very best version of Self, because in doing so, that's when I become the very best version of myself. In those moments I am unlocking the greatest secret and mystery of the Universe. LOVE.

Breakthrough #12

The Platinum Rule . . . and Your Emotional Spoke

One of the most important aspects of self-awareness is understanding our EMOTIONAL SPOKE. This Spoke is about our emotional states and how we manage them. It includes how we feel about ourselves, the people we care about, and the events and circumstances of our lives.

We spend much of our lives being stimulated by emotions, but we often don't take the time to recognize them, understand why they are present, integrate them, and use their energy effectively.

E-motion is simply "energy in motion"

We tend to think of certain emotions as being "good" or "bad"—we want more of the ones that make us feel good—and others, we want to avoid.

However, energy cannot inherently be "good" or "bad." It's just information. (See BREAKTHROUGH #10.) What we are wanting to avoid is how those emotions make us feel in our body.

The energy or "charge" of emotions can create a conscious or unconscious "drive" to take action.

This energy can also be used to manipulate others into action—a skill which the advertising industry uses to make us buy things we don't need.

However, any emotion—even challenging ones—can also be used to "inspire" positive actions. This BREAKTHROUGH is one that great leaders and statesmen throughout history have mastered.

• • • • • • • • • • • • • • • • • • •

When I was ten years old, one day my mom told me that I should act more "gentlemanly-like" when they had important guests over for their posh business dinners.

I remember feeling confused and inadequate. Clearly I was doing something wrong. My shame and embarrassment around not knowing what to do was also tinged with anger and defensiveness. How was I supposed to know this stuff without being taught? After all, I was only a kid! Whenever something like this happened, it triggered a core belief that there must be something wrong with ME!

Since expressing feelings wasn't encouraged in our home—and boys couldn't show vulnerability—I simply decided to ask my dad how to become more "gentlemanly-like." I had often heard other women comment to my mom what a "gentleman" my dad was, so that seemed like a good plan.

His reply was lovely. He said, "Well, you just act as if you are a gentleman, and then one day, after you have practiced it long enough, you won't think about it and you will just be a gentleman." He never was long on "how-to"s, but I got the point and actually observed him in action for clues and tips and ideas. It's what some people call "fake it till you make it." Actually, it was rather fun acting up and getting the reactions I got.

My dad was such a charmer with women, and quite charismatic. But the number one word that sticks in my mind when I think back on observing him for clues and tips and ideas about his "gentlemanliness" with women, is the word "interested."

He listened attentively and was, apparently, genuinely interested in whatever it was he asked them about. He would rarely tell a story about himself to reciprocate his own "interestingness" until the woman he was talking to felt completely heard and understood and appreciated and acknowledged.

However, I noticed that with men he could brag and try to impress. This made me squirm. Thinking about it as I was writing this chapter, I realized why he behaved this way. It is because his own dad was away in World War II for five years during Dad's early teens, and he only had his mom at home for company—a pattern that was repeated in my own life with him being away so much during my growing up years. I always felt a need to impress him, to get his attention. I worked with my business partner, Jennifer, and made a BREAKTHROUGH by getting this behavior repatterned! (See BREAKTHROUGH #10.)

Most people have similar experiences in their childhood that triggered core emotional patterns and associated beliefs. What's important is whether we are still reacting to events in our adult life in the way we reacted as children.

> **Are you aware of the emotions you are feeling at any particular time and why?**

> **Do you recognize the links between these emotions and how you behave?**

> **Are you aware of the impact that your emotions—and reactions— can have on others?**

There's nothing wrong with feeling emotions. It's how we express and communicate them that counts.

When unresolved patterns from childhood are played out in the workplace, they can affect the performance of others—and be detrimental to your career and long-term success.

Think of the highly-strung person who gets angry at everyone in the office for a seemingly trivial reason and then leaves the room and goes back to his or her job, unaware of the fact that he or she may have ruined the performance of the rest of the team for the next week. People who suppress their anger (or other emotions such as sadness, fear, shock, resentment or disgust), and who may be less overt in their emotional expression, while less easy to spot, can have equally devastating effects on the performance of themselves and others.

Having awareness of emotional states, both within ourselves—and others—is critical.

Knowing how to handle your emotions effectively is important, as they can have a huge impact on ourselves and on others. Unless we learn how to "respond" in the face of any nonresourceful emotions— whether our own, or those of others—we can effectively be hijacked into "reactions" that frustrate our best intentions.

While we may not be able to prevent challenging emotional responses from occurring—we can develop the Emotional Intelligence (EQ) to deal with them appropriately and in ways that are not harmful to ourselves or damaging to relationships with those around us.

Developing Emotional Intelligence (EQ) is fundamental to achieving almost every BREAKTHROUGH in this book.

Long before I heard the term "Emotional Intelligence," there was what my mom called "The Golden Rule," **"Treat others as you yourself would like to be treated."** In other words, if you want to be spoken to respectfully and treated with consideration, then you should treat others that way. (Years later, I figured out that that's probably why Dad learned to show interest in women—and so did I—because we wanted our mothers to show that same level of interest in us! But I digress . . .)

The Golden Rule works to some degree—but it also has its limitations.

I remember many years ago coming home from work on a Friday evening and presenting my then girlfriend, Tania, with some flowers I had bought for her at the florist on the way home. I liked fresh flowers for the weekend and I was sure she would, too. I particularly liked a purple and yellow combination (and still do!) and so that's what I bought. And because I'd had a good week and was in a good mood, I brought an extra-big bouquet.

I was underwhelmed by the nonreaction as the cellophane wrapping was ripped off and thrown into the trash, a vase (but not a suitable one) was half-filled with water and the flowers were dumped into the vase while Tania went off to do something else—without even a thank you.

Feeling upset, miffed, surprised, irritated, confused, rejected, whatever . . . I asked her what was wrong.

"You didn't buy those flowers for me . . . you bought them for you. I don't like yellow flowers, as you should know by now, I only like red and white ones. And if you look in the lounge, there is already a big bouquet of yellow and purple flowers there that I bought earlier for *you*!"

Ooops!

I learned that the Golden Rule doesn't really work, because it only works if the other person wants what you want. In fact, it's actually a selfish rule.

What works much better is:

Treat others as THEY would have you treat THEM.

That's what I call the PLATINUM RULE.

I remember another gift from Tania—in the same category—which was when she told me that women are much more attracted to men who are "interested" rather than "interesting."

I have observed that, in general, people treat us in the way that we teach them to treat us. And if we treat them the way they would like us to treat them, guess what? They will do the same for us!

The best "how to" guide to the Platinum Rule that I have ever seen is contained in Gary Chapman's wonderful book, *The Five Love Languages*. I am grateful for his permission to quote him directly here:

Words of Affirmation

Actions don't always speak louder than words. If this is your love language, unsolicited compliments mean the world to you. Hearing the words, "I love you," are important—hearing the reasons behind that love sends your spirits skyward. Insults can leave you shattered and are not easily forgotten.

Quality Time

In the vernacular of Quality Time, nothing says, "I love you," like full, undivided attention. Being there for this type of person is critical, but really being there—with the TV off, fork and knife down, and all chores and tasks on standby—makes your significant other feel truly special and loved. Distractions, postponed dates, or the failure to listen can be especially hurtful.

Receiving Gifts

Don't mistake this love language for materialism; the receiver of gifts thrives on the love, thoughtfulness, and effort behind the gift. If you speak this language, the perfect gift or gesture shows that you are known, you are cared for, and you are prized above whatever was sacrificed to bring the gift to you. A missed birthday, anniversary, or a hasty, thoughtless gift would be disastrous—so would the absence of everyday gestures.

Acts of Service

Can vacuuming the floors really be an expression of love? Absolutely! Anything you do to ease the burden of responsibilities weighing on an "Acts of Service" person will speak volumes. The words he or she most want to hear: "Let me do that for you." Laziness, broken commitments, and making more work for them tell speakers of this language their feelings don't matter.

Physical Touch

This language isn't all about the bedroom. A person whose primary language is Physical Touch is, not surprisingly, very touchy. Hugs, pats on the back, holding hands, and thoughtful touches on the arm, shoulder, or face—they can all be ways to show excitement, concern, care, and love. Physical presence and accessibility are crucial, while neglect or abuse can be unforgivable and destructive.

The Five Love Languages book includes a fun quiz at the back that you can take to find out what your love language stack ranking is; i.e., which of these five is most important to you, and which is least, and how they rank from one to five.

I remember doing this exercise with my family. All five of us had a different preferred Love Language. We laughed and cried tears of joy as we shared fascinating examples of what really worked (and didn't work) for each of us. It was a wonderfully intimate conversation, where we all genuinely cared about one another's various responses.

It's certainly a much more fun and interesting way to spend an evening than numbing ourselves watching mindless television or on Facebook!

Learning to communicate with our loved ones and those significant people in our lives in a way that works for them—and for us—has to be one of the greatest BREAKTHROUGH areas there is. It creates real joy and magic. We are in FLOW! We feel PLEASED and SHINING.

Communicating with others about our emotions—and our needs—in a way that is mutually satisfying and productive isn't as natural or easy as it sounds, however.

We filter everything we hear through values and beliefs that often bear no resemblance to the values and beliefs (or filters) of the person communicating with us. And based on our understanding (and frequently, not understanding) that communication—we have an emotional response.

In addition, many people grow up in homes or cultures where expressing emotions isn't acceptable, or isn't encouraged, or where certain emotions are taboo. Communicating our emotions—and being fully present when others communicate their emotions—is an EQ skill that is never too late to learn. Honing and improving that skill in our interactions with people in both our personal and professional life is an ongoing journey.

There is a simple and powerful technique, which I call MVE, that can cut out so much unnecessary confusion and unintended miscommunication between two people. It involves three simple steps:

Mirroring

Validating

Empathizing

The MVE technique can apply to conversations between lovers, or parent and child, as much as between boss and coworker. It is an effective way to communicate deeply and bring greater understanding—and we all want to be understood. Being understood motivates us to perform to a higher level and helps us identify how we can support ourselves and others to do the best job possible—and be the best possible version of Self.

MVE serves a number of vital functions in the creation of "conscious" communication. I've elected to use the simple example of a male-female partner relationship. However, the process can be applied equally in any interaction between two people.

First, MIRRORING focuses attention on the actual words being spoken. Most of us rarely listen to what other people are actually saying. When we should be listening, what we are really doing is reacting and responding to the impact on us of what we are hearing; i.e., we are listening to ourselves react. When the focus is on the other's actual words, there is a much better chance that the intended message has been received, because there is more of a chance of getting to the meaning behind the words.

Second, when you truly, deeply listen and search for meaning with the other in a dialogue, you can discover that your partner's experience or reality is very different from your own much of the time.

Third, using the MVE technique creates a deep emotional connection. When a dialogue reaches this profound level, it becomes a spiritual experience. (Matthew Kelly's book *The Seven Levels of Intimacy* is a must read on this topic.)

In the MIRRORING technique, we replay what we think we heard and ask the other, "Did I get it?"

Example: Person A and Person B

> A: I don't enjoy cooking supper for you when you don't appreciate the effort I put in. Do you understand?

> B: Let me see if I have understood. You don't enjoy cooking supper every night for me when I don't show you appreciation for all the effort you have put in. Is that correct?

This process is repeated as many times as is required until Person A tells Person B:

> A: You have now fully understood my issue.

At this point, Person B will ask:

> B: Is there more?

Person A might embellish on the original point by saying something like:

> A: I feel deflated when you eat without ever remarking or commenting. It takes hours to prepare and I always attempt to make it look attractive.

This "tell me more" part of MIRRORING is the key. Person A will feel both HEARD and UNDERSTOOD. And it creates a strong emotional bond both ways. Although you might be thinking that it sounds easy, believe me, it's not. It's so contrary to the way most couples interact that it can take a lot of practice. It's also, as one client recently attested after trying this out, "a complete and unexpected luxury to have (my partner's) full attention."

Now that you have cracked mirroring (no pun intended), let's step up and move on to VALIDATING. This is the stage where you both learn to affirm the internal logic of each other's remarks. In essence, what you are saying to each other is, "What you are saying makes sense to me and I can see why you would think that way."

Because our two most basic needs are to be HEARD and UNDERSTOOD, the use of validating and mirroring is very powerful.

A few weeks ago I ended up chatting with a client and her husband about the MVE method. They'd had a disagreement over something minor that had spilled over into World War III. I asked her, "What is it you want from him that you are not being given?"

"I want him to tell me that I am not crazy and that I make sense."

My client wanted more than just to be heard. She wanted to be understood, to have her thought process validated. She wanted her husband to tell her that her worldview made sense. I know them both well and asked him if he was open to a new idea—MVE? After an hour, the three-way facilitated conversation went something like this.

A: Do you agree with me?

B: I do not agree.

A: But does what I'm saying make sense? Am I crazy?

B: No, you are not crazy—but I don't agree with you still.

A: Does what I am saying make sense?

B: Yes, it does. And I can understand why you would think and feel like that.

A: That's all I wanted to hear! It's fine to disagree, but it's not been fine feeling I was crazy and didn't make sense.

Both of them were protecting their separate realities for fear of "losing themselves."

The inner dialogue was: "If I see it your way, that feels like I can't see it my way. If I can feel your feelings, that invalidates mine. If what you say is true, then what I say must be false. There can only be one center of the universe. And guess what? It's mine!"

By suspending for a few moments the view that theirs was the only center of the universe, something magical happened. First, they both felt SAFE. Second, they lowered their defenses and were willing to embrace some of the other's perception of reality. To their mutual surprise, the drawbridge was lowered—a hug offered—and a sense of REAL CONNECTION felt.

And all because they had followed the Platinum Rule.

So practice containing your instinctual "reaction" to someone else's words, which is so often to defend and then counter attack—and "respond" instead using MIRRORING and VALIDATING.

And there's one more piece . . . if MIRRORING is the cake and VALIDATING is the icing—then the cherry on the top is EMPATHY.

An empathic response may sound something like:

> "Given the fact that you see things the way you do, it makes sense to me that you would feel upset. I can imagine you were confused and upset."

It's complete Venus and Mars stereotyping rubbish, in my view, to say that men are all about logic and women are all about feelings. For the woman in the earlier example, the validation of her thought process was more important than the validation of her feelings; but for others, the affirmation of their emotions makes them feel whole and loved. For anyone familiar with the MBTI profiling tool, I suspect this difference is more reflective of T(hinking) and F(eeling) types.

Regardless of gender, or personality type, if anger between two people is "heard" and acknowledged—and there is empathy—it can be resolved and will dissipate.

Empathy is the key to healing in many situations. It can be broken down into four steps that anyone can learn and put into practice:

Listen actively to what the person is actually saying.

Demonstrate an awareness of how the other is feeling.

Accurately **identify** the underlying cause of another person's perspective.

Express an understanding of the other person's perspective.

Mastering the Platinum Rule and MVE both require practicing Empathy–having an awareness of what the other is experiencing.

Think of someone with whom you could have a real BREAKTHROUGH by practicing the PLATINUM RULE or MVE!

Now go and apply it!

Breakthrough #13

Health Matters . . .
Your Physical Spoke

Smoking kills! It says so in large letters on the side of the pack.

How many more lectures from my kids, or gory articles or documentaries, did I need to see and hear to make me stop? For more than 20 years I had smoked 20-plus cigarettes a day. I wasn't addicted. I was stupid!

So, on March 7, 2001, I went to see a hypnotherapist to help me quit. He asked me a hundred questions about my smoking habits, from what time of day I had my first one to what I liked about that particular one that was different from the second one . . . why with coffee, why with wine, which ones I didn't like, where I smoked, etc. So many questions!

Ninety minutes into my hypnotherapy session, he was still on a roll with more questions . . . every one of which, I have to admit, really did make me think about my smoking habit in a completely conscious way that I never had before. I decided to brave asking him the question, "Are you actually going to hypnotize me?"

To my complete surprise, he explained why he didn't need to. In his opinion, I wasn't actually addicted to nicotine, I was addicted to a pattern. Sound familiar?

He asked me when the last time was that I hadn't had an alcoholic drink all day.

Somewhat sheepishly, I said, "About 20 years ago, I guess."

"No, seriously," he replied.

"Yes, seriously," I replied.

He asked me, "So, do you think you could go a day without alcohol?"

I laughed out loud. "You think I'm an alcoholic, don't you? Look, I have worked with a few; I know what an alcoholic looks like and I'm not one."

He asked me again. "So, do you think you could go a day without alcohol?"

"Of course!"

"Two days?"

"Definitely!"

"A week?"

"No problem!" . . . and so on.

Eventually I blurted out, "Look, if it will help me give up smoking, I'll quit for ten years."

He said, "I bet you can't."

I said, "F@%# you!" (Well, I thought it, at least.) Then shook hands. Paid the fee. Walked out. I'd show him.

For more than ten years after that, not one drop of alcohol passed my lips—or coffee (as it too was associated in my mind with the same pattern)—and most important, not one cigarette.

Although I have never taken up smoking again, I do now drink coffee—and love it—and have rekindled my old interest in drinking a glass or two of wine with a nice meal.

When someone doesn't drink alcohol in social settings, most people make assumptions. They'll often inquire whether you're an alcoholic (or that's what they'll be thinking, even if they don't say it!). The phrase "I don't drink alcohol" opens up more conversations about the other person's "stuff" than you ever wanted to know or thought possible based on four simple words.

I once experimented with saying "I don't like sex" to see whether it generated the same response. It didn't! I just got to hear lots of sad stories from the person I was chatting to about how they used to like sex, but now had a pretty hopeless or nonexistent sex life (that's a subject for another book, I think!).

Of the six Spokes in The Wheel of Life, there is no doubt in my mind that PHYSICAL is the BIG Daddy. The primus inter pares—or first among equals.

Being the very best version of ourselves PHYSICALLY involves a short list of nonnegotiable daily disciplines.

For me, as for most people, they involve DIET, EXERCISE, SLEEP and WATER.

I know everyone is different in terms of the amount of sleep that they say they need in order to function well, but for me it's seven hours. Not six and a half or seven and a half—but seven! I can survive on less, but I don't function optimally.

Getting quality sleep is very much underrated as an essential ingredient in overall health. It allows our body to restore and heal itself on autopilot. It allows our 100 trillion (that's 100,000,000,000,000) cells to do their work.

It sounds strange, but every night when I go to sleep, I say to those cells, "Body, heal thyself." And they do!

I don't think it's just because they're young and innocent that young children sleep like logs, wake up fresh and bursting with energy, with clear minds, happy, healthy and raring to go. I think a lot of that has to do with being free from worry and stress, as well as free from much of the negative programming that we accumulate along the way to adulthood.

Rather than proclaim how tired we are, or that we can put on weight by simply looking at food (the "see food" diet!), it's wiser to give our body positive messages like, "I feel so full of energy," "I sleep like a log," "I enjoy a glass of wine with my food," and, "As long as I eat sensibly, I can eat whatever I like."

The things we fear and dread are drawn to us in just the same way as positive things are—through our thoughts, words and actions. It's the Law of Attraction at work again. The placebo effect is proof enough of the power of belief.

Think of strength and power and vibrant health, and you will draw it toward you. Dwell on your ailment and watch yourself take twice as long to recover (if you do) than someone with the first mindset.

Your body listens to what you think and feel and say—and responds accordingly. Illness is about energetic dissonance (or disease) and I have come to learn and understand that the natural energy field within us is the true healer of *all* illness and disease.

When it comes to managing my weight and dieting, I have learned this. If I eat more calories than I burn off, I gain weight. If I burn off more calories than I consume, I lose weight. I know that I need to keep an eye on this and so I do. But I also tell myself, "I can eat whatever I like, whenever I like, as long as I'm sensible."

Being the best version of myself means making sensible decisions around food. It means that I need to make saying "no" to having a particular thing to eat or drink, the same as saying "yes" to a higher purpose—like maintaining the body shape I want (I'm grateful to Matthew Kelly for this distinction).

This concept, that saying "no" to something can mean saying "yes" to a higher purpose, can be applied to everything from choosing what we put into our body—to relationships.

When it comes to health and well-being, different bodies, personalities, and metabolic types respond to different things, especially when it comes to achieving or maintaining one's ideal body weight. I've found one holistic eating plan that works for my body. It's called the Zone Diet. Beyond simply counting calories, it teaches you to combine the correct ratios of healthy carbohydrates, proteins and fats required by the body—and to ingest them at regular intervals throughout the day to optimize your biochemistry.

And why does this work? It has to do with all of those millions and millions of eicosanoids flying around your system. These super-hormones are signaling molecules (made from EFAs, or essential fatty acids) that control other hormones and, in fact, most bodily systems, including your nervous and immune systems. They do all this despite the fact that their life span is somewhere between seconds and minutes.

So that old adage, "You are what you eat," still holds true!

In discovering and designing the optimal health practices for yourself, bear in mind that . . .

Health—the holistic state where all body systems, from nervous to muscular to digestive, circulatory, skeletal, hormonal, muscular, etc., are all working together optimally . . . and

Fitness–the physical ability to perform various athletic activities

. . . are *not* the same thing.

So, finally, here's my advice about exercise–do it–and do it regularly!

What are your Goals in terms of a BREAKTHROUGH in your health?

Remember . . . health matters!

Breakthrough #14

Gratitude Generates Greatness . . . Your Spiritual Spoke

During my teenage years, I knew exactly what I wanted to do when I left school. I wanted to be James Bond. Not only was I attracted by the obvious benefits of the job (the girls, the cars, the toys, the attire), I was also attracted by the "007" style (suave, sophisticated, smart, strong, sporty) and his purpose (to save the world from bad guys and tyrants).

For years I thought of little else. I studied languages and took my sports and physical fitness very seriously. I applied to join the British Army and wanted to learn to fly a helicopter. The army would sponsor me to go to a college, and I was looking forward to playing rugby and other sports at the highest level.

At age 16, just two years away from going to college, I received some news that was a huge shock. I was told that I needed an operation on my left hip. It was a rather serious operation that entailed inserting metal screws, pins and plates—and then having another round of surgery a year later to remove them all.

For reasons that were never adequately explained to me, my parents determined that it was better that I didn't discover the implications of this surgery until after the operation—indeed, some two months after the operation, when the huge plaster cast was removed.

As a result of this operation, I would not be allowed to join the army—and therefore could never become James Bond!

I had no plan B. Indeed, now I didn't even have a plan A!

It was around that time that I first heard the John Lennon lyric about "life being what happens to us when we are busy making other plans" and it really spoke to me.

This was also the time when I encountered my first ever mentor—Sister McCullough, who headed up the orthopedic ward I was in for the three weeks after the operation. It was she who taught me that the right "attitude" would help me achieve the BREAKTHROUGH I needed.

Many years later, it became clear to me that this turn of events in my life was the catalyst for my "spiritual awakening."

My convalescence gave me time to think and create a new plan. I started to think about who I was, what I really wanted—and what I truly wanted to do with my life. My thoughts turned to how I could travel, use my languages, and make a difference in the world in ways other than through joining the army.

How was it that I found the strength within me to turn around what was potentially a negative situation—while the guy in the bed next to me was still in the hospital a year later when I went back to have the metalwork removed? Sadly, he was about to lose his leg as a result of having developed gangrene.

Sister McCullough was of the opinion that he had the "wrong attitude" and that his experience was "Nature's way of giving him what he had attracted with his attitude."

Why do I share this story? From that time on, I knew intuitively that "spirituality" was important, but I didn't really know how to describe it, spend time on it, or how to further develop it.

I've since learned that the body has an innate wisdom and that it gives us information through pain, injuries and other imbalances in our system. Pain is the body's way of trying to tell us something. Taking medication can numb the pain (the symptom), but unless we become aware of, and deal with, the root cause, the problem will persist, recur, and, over time, possibly deteriorate. (See BREAKTHROUGHs #9 and #10.)

Pain or "disease" in your body can be a doorway to a BREAKTHROUGH.

One of the things that I've learned over the years is that spirituality is totally personal, but in essence it means **spending quality time devoted to living our life purpose**, whatever that is.

Having the awareness that you are alive for some purpose, and discovering how that purpose can be lived in the present, is absolutely vital if you're golng to achieve the BREAKTHROUGH of having a spiritually rich and fulfilled life.

It doesn't need to be any more complex than this.

Spirituality needs to be part of the daily routine of our life. We need to find time every day for some solitude in which we can meditate or reflect—some time when we can be with ourselves, connect within, and ponder life's big questions, such as:

Who am I?

How am I doing?

Am I living in accordance with my values?

Am I living in accordance with my life's purpose?

Am I being the best version of myself?

Over the course of many years, I've learned the way that works best for me is to do a short eight-minute meditation twice every day. I'm not suggesting this routine will work for everyone. However some of my (extremely busy!) clients have successfully adopted (and also adapted) this strategy in a way that sits in alignment with their personal beliefs and cosmology.

Here's how it works. My alarm goes off at 7:00 a.m. and I hit the snooze button. This gives me exactly eight minutes to do a **gratitude meditation** before getting out of bed to start my day. What this involves is literally thinking through the things I am grateful for in my life.

They might be things that happened the day before, or on the weekend. They can be contemporary things or macro things. I focus on whatever it is I'm grateful for in that moment.

One of the most important things I've learned is that even the things that we think are "bad" (i.e., not as we would have liked them to work out) always contain something to be grateful for.

For example, when I'm asked about the demise of my last marriage, I always say I am "sad but glad." Who wouldn't be sad to end a relationship with someone they loved?

And yet I'm also glad, because I'm grateful for some wonderful things that happened in that relationship. And I'm also grateful for receiving the opportunity to learn about my Self, and what I really need in a relationship and In lIfe—things, I discovered, that this relationship was never going to provide. Therefore, I'm grateful for what I can take forward.

> **We can find something to be grateful for in everything—even in what appears to be a "problem."**

The last thing I do at night before I go to sleep is another short meditation that I call my **aligning meditation**. During this time, I reflect on my day and ask, "What did I do today that helped me become the best version of myself?"

In thinking about my day and what I've achieved, I also reflect on whether I could have done those things any better—and whether there's anything else I need to focus on tomorrow to become an even better version of myself.

I think having a little bit of solitude or quiet time, where you just reflect on how you are doing and how aligned you are with your lifestyle, is a great daily discipline.

The other thing, which is absolutely mission-critical for achieving BREAKTHROUGHs, is that, at least once a year (or twice a year, ideally), we should take periods of complete solitude. It might be 24 hours, 48 hours, or longer, but this is about getting away from *everything* that is in our regular environment. It's time to detach and unhook from everything and everybody, to go within and find our center, and to make space for whatever wants or needs to emerge to do so.

Meditation is probably too "posh" a word for what I do. And however much I practice, it doesn't get easier. My mind still goes all over the place at times, but that doesn't mean I stop doing it or that I don't find it useful.

When I count my blessings each day and feel gratitude, when I "check in" and feel appreciation for all that I have going for me, it makes me smile. The sun shines inside me. The music in my head makes me feel alive and at peace. I feel full of grace, strength, courage and confidence.

Each day, I set the intention to give more than I get, to deliver more than I was paid for, and to exceed people's expectations. I do my best and go the extra mile. This helps me to enjoy the rewards I receive even more.

I accept that I've made mistakes and a few serious blunders—and may continue to do so. I accept that I can't win every time—and I can still always do my best.

I test my limits to see what it takes for me to give up. I work hard. I am diligent. But I also take time to learn—and to reflect.

I reflect on my actions and what they say to me and to others about the best version of my Self . . .

Did I achieve my intended outcomes?

Did I make a difference?

Did I take myself too seriously?

Did I laugh at myself? And at life?

Did I major on minor things?

Did I neglect the little touches that make such a difference?

Did I smile?

Did I move closer to the things on my Goals Poster—and on my Bucket List? (See BREAKTHROUGH #16 and TOOL #13)

Did I open my mind and heart to new opportunities and possibilities?

Did I find happiness within me? Did I share? Hug? Serve?

Did I learn something?

What did I decide?

Every day I aim to do all of these things—to the best of my abilities.

This is my daily spiritual practice. You must find your own.

Without some kind of daily discipline, this Spiritual Spoke can sabotage the rest of your journey at some point in time.

Eating badly or drinking too much is sustainable for a short period, but not forever. The same applies to lack of sleep or exercise. It's no different with attending to your Spirit and your Soul.

To achieve BREAKTHROUGHs in our Spiritual Spoke, we need to "adjust" our attitude to one of gratitude. We need to continue to check in regularly and ask . . .

Is there anything else I can do—or that I can do better?

. . . and LISTEN for the answers that come back from that highest and best version of Self.

Breakthrough #15

Living in The Zone . . . Your Professional Spoke

Are you making a living doing something that plays to your strengths, develops your gifts, provides opportunities for you to grow and learn—and that most of all enables you to become the best version of yourself?

This is the focus of the PROFESS-IONAL SPOKE in the Wheel of Life.

Let's say we work a ten-hour day (including commute time) and then spend roughly ten hours at home in the evenings (eating dinner, getting ready for bed, sleeping seven or eight hours, and then getting ready for work again!)—that leaves only around four hours a day for "life."

So on most days, we spend about twice as much time at work as we do in our personal life.

On that basis, wouldn't it be better to "make a living" doing something that you love and feel passionate about?

In researching which areas of life most people wanted to achieve BREAKTHROUGHs in, I've learned that younger people place CAREER at the top of their list without any hesitation.

These days it's close to impossible for a young working person to buy an apartment, or even rent one, in most major cities, on salary alone.

For college graduates, it's often financially crippling or even impossible for them to pay off their student loans—especially when there are so few jobs to be had after graduation. And for those who do find employment, it's rarely in the field they are qualified in.

When young people now look at their parents' (my) generation, they wonder why we've created a world in which it seems impossible for them to climb above the first rung on the ladder, let alone achieve success and thrive.

Aside from caring for themselves and their aging parents, many in my generation now have the additional burden of providing support for their disadvantaged children.

There is already so much conflict in the World between the "haves" and the "have-nots." As this kind of tension begins to spread within family generations, it will fracture communities, and in a worst-case scenario, would fuel even more social unrest than we currently have. The occasional ugly squabbles that can erupt within families over an inheritance or family business will look tame by comparison!

Of even greater concern is that many countries are experiencing "springs" and "events" that involve social upheaval and violence, the consequences of which we cannot yet fully envisage–and therefore we are far from properly prepared.

My intention is that BREAKTHROUGH and my mentoring work will serve to assist my children's generation (young people in their twenties), so that they will not be the first in the economic history of developed nations to earn less than the previous generation and to accumulate less wealth–placing a further burden on governments and society in the future.

I believe that the only way that the Millennials will be able to compete and win in the future is to find their North Star, to find meaning and purpose in life, and have a career BREAKTHROUGH in what I call THE BREAKTHROUGH ZONE.

Some years ago, I developed a simple formula to illustrate this.

The ideal is to find a job, career or vocation that is at the intersection of these four circles–in the BREAKTHROUGH ZONE!

If you study highly successful people, they are all operating at the intersection of these four circles–operating in THE ZONE. This applies as much to leaders in business, as to legends in the arts and entertainment fields.

I guarantee that if you don't find a job that takes you into THE ZONE and keeps you there, it won't be too long before you are either fired– or resign. When you live out of alignment with your highest potential and the best version of yourself, that lack of coherence continues

to show up in the events of your life, demanding resolution. (See BREAKTHROUGH #10.)

What exactly is THE ZONE?

The Zone is that place where it all connects and comes together and you are "in FLOW" and it feels PERFECT. Finding the work that feels like play for you will turn you from an underachiever into a happy hero warrior.

I admire Mihály Csikszentmiháyli's research into the positive aspects of the human experience and the joy, creativity and process of total involvement with life, which he calls FLOW. Being in The Zone is being "in flow" in our careers. To quote him:

"Flow is the state of mind when consciousness is harmoniously ordered and [people] want to pursue whatever they are doing for its own sake."

Being in The Zone happens when our energy is focused on realistic goals and when our gifts and skills match the opportunity for achieving the results that we desire.

We love facing challenges that we know we can overcome, that involve using our skills and talents, and that require the kind of total focus that causes us to forget everything and everyone else and completely lose ourselves in the task.

If we can find—and live in—the ZONE, we have the potential for much higher levels of achievement and happiness.

• • • • • • • • • • • • • • • • • • • •

TED is a nonprofit organization that brings together people from Technology, Education and Design for educational talks, and their motto is, "Ideas Worth Spreading." At one of their events a few years ago, Sir Ken Robinson told a wonderful story about a girl in a drawing class at kindergarten. Normally, this little girl didn't pay attention, but in the art class she was engrossed. The teacher found this fascinating and asked the girl what she was drawing. She replied that she was drawing a picture of God. "But nobody knows what God looks like," the teacher tried to explain. The little girl said, "They will in a minute."

I love the message contained in this story, as it's similar to the story about my daughter, Rosie, and the way all the children in her kindergarten class believed in their singing ability.

It saddens me that we have the ability to turn people "off," "down" or "out" by simply telling them that they can't sing, or draw, or do whatever it is that they want to do. Or by telling them that their lives will come to naught.

As a result of such put-downs, very few people ever connect with their deepest talents. Without a real sense of what your talents and passions are, you will never enjoy what you are doing, or have any idea about your actual potential, or how to get there. Without knowing what you are capable of, you can't know what your highest potential is—or could be—and thus achieve the BREAKTHROUGH of being the best version of yourself.

This is a tragedy for the individual—and also for our society.

Self-belief is vital for sustainable success in the PROFESSIONAL SPOKE. It also requires a determination to succeed within your chosen field—one that puts you in The Zone.

Most highly successful people who are in The Zone didn't pursue their passions because of the promise of a paycheck. They found their Zone, then practiced and perfected their expertise for 10,000 hours or more.

Peak performers in The Zone not only demonstrate passion—they have the right attitude. Their mojo is working. They have a natural aptitude for their chosen vocation and an intuitive grasp of their gift and how to apply it. But they don't take their gifts for granted—they continue to hone their skills and improve their performance.

They know in what way they are intelligent. They understand that their intelligence is a combination of intellectual, gut and heart intelligence, and in The Zone they synthesize these diverse, dynamic and distinctive gifts in new ways that achieve BREAKTHROUGH results that set them apart.

They know who they can become because they know what they can do—and they take a deep delight in doing it. They simply can't imagine doing anything else.

What sets them apart from others is a driving need to break through to their highest potential, to become the best version of themselves. Nothing less will do.

Those who live in The Zone are endlessly curious and congregate with others who are in the same groove to learn from them and see what's new and happening in their chosen specialization.

They understand that they can change their world and their future by changing their attitude. This is their real power and what sustains their mojo.

They often enjoy the fame and the fortune that accompany such success, but mostly they thrive on being in the game because they're having so much fun. Regardless of the financial rewards, it's the sense of authenticity, freedom and independence they have achieved that they love—and no price can be put on those. There's nothing else they'd rather be doing.

Others often consider peak performers "lucky" . . . but their luck is self-created from perseverance, self-belief, optimism and ambition.

Never set aside what would put you in The Zone for the sake of financial security. Excuses like, "I need to stay in this (lousy) job to pay the mortgage" are not sustainable.

Be connected with your sense of identity, purpose and well-being—and allow it to guide everything you do in your life.

You might wait a long time for a "lucky break"—you can make this BREAKTHROUGH any time.

Locating your ZONE

You don't just land in The Zone. You need to hold it as a vision and then walk toward it. As you get nearer, you start to run. And once you begin to run, like Joan of Arc, you'll never look back.

The key to locating The Zone is finding your distinctive talents and passions.

The world's population doubled in the last 50 years and is heading from 7 billion today toward 9 billion in the next 50 years. This explosion in humanity will use technology that doesn't exist today in ways we haven't ever imagined or thought possible.

Standing out from the crowd in the future will be a major factor that determines who gets the work, and therefore paid and fed, and who does not!

We are all born with extraordinary powers of imagination, creativity, intelligence, intuition, spirituality and physical or sensory awareness, but end up using only a fraction of these gifts—and some not at all.

Identifying and figuring out how to apply your unique strengths and gifts is not something that's "nice to have." It's an absolute "need to have" for surviving and thriving. It's making ourselves "future proof."

Those dormant skills you have will be very valuable one day.

Understanding our potential unlocks genius.

Utilizing our unique gifts and skills in The Zone builds the foundation for a fulfilling, happy and successful future.

. . . .

A few years ago I was introduced to an interesting exercise that's easy to do and very revealing about our hidden and not-so-hidden talents, skills and gifts. It's called THE STREAM and it goes like this.

Begin by writing your full name followed by the word "is," i.e.,

David Carter is ....

And then just go for it! Write and write and write and write and write. Like a stream. Let it flow and keep flowing. Think of all of your roles and relationships and find words that describe you and your qualities, gifts, skills and talents within those roles and situations. Ask ten friends to help you. Ask your boss, your partner, your parents and your kids. But most of all, ask yourself:

What do I know about myself that no one else ever sees?

I did this exercise on and off for a period of a week—writing, adding, sharing, collecting and collating. I asked many other people for their feedback and observations to include. It was fascinating.

Here's what I ended up with.

Free spirit, quick thinker, quick mover, independent, autonomous, rule breaker, fearless, generous, decisive, certain, positive attitude, spokes balanced (PMSEPP), fun, cheeky, serious, committed, curious, sincere, storyteller, a metaphor creator, visionary, articulate, spiritual, intuitive, on a journey, on a quest, where I live is important to me, proper selfishness, we teach the things we most want to learn, when the student is ready the teacher appears, the wisdom is always within, life always presents learning opportunities at precisely the right time, authentic, "what's really going on?" sheepdog, shepherd, intimate, trusting, trustworthy, keen on fitness, vain, tidy, orderly, neat, a partner in a partnership (work and home), going with the flow, energy sensitive, enjoying being me, inspirational, motivational, good listener, insightful, results-orientated, INFP, make myself useful, personal developer (self and others), discerning, sense of identity, fearful of injustice/rejection/ punishment/neglect, emotionally aware, emotionally open, committed father, friend (a good one), honest, charismatic, decent, amusing, integrity, intelligent, dyslexic, excited by the possibility, purposeful, powerful, masterful, a learner, I desire to be loved unconditionally for who I am, home is where my toothbrush is, golfer, loyal, chef, affectionate, affirming, appreciative, maverick, enigma, open, thoughtful, kind, considerate, generous with time/money/attention/ network, action-orientated, spontaneous, pottering, meticulous, controlling, demanding, striving for excellence in all I do, romantic, film lover, emotional, conscious, road tripper/driver, music lover, aesthete, an epicure, strong-willed, genuine, committed to living life fully, a connector, networker, salesman, mentor, coach, guru, Yoda, therapist, Luke Skywalker, imaginative, big-picture thinker, introverted, shy, patient, quiet, chatty, laughter lover, tears crier, thorough, well dressed, clean, groomed, organized, one-step-at-a-time, fully alive, a Border Collie lover, resourceful, warm weather lover, west-facing sunset-over-ocean-view lover, explorer, unconventional, agreeable, reserved, reflective, private, depth and focus vs. spread thin and various, observant, perceptive, self-managing, self-motivated, independent, self-sufficient, self-disciplined, confident, even-tempered, don't carry grudges, low ego, capable, effective, low stress, calm, at peace, proud, honorable, a man of my word, loyal, verbose!

I don't share this list as any kind of suggested ideal target. Indeed, as I reflect on its contents, I see the "big picture," the paradoxes and opposites—and also some areas for improvement. Where others might see chaos, feel triggered, or make judgments or comparisons as they read the list, my response is simply to smile—and to laugh at myself.

The thing is, this is my list. It's what makes me unique. Doing this exercise helped me understand more about who I am and to believe in my Self. I feel alive and in The Zone when I bring all of these talents and passions together in the service of others, helping them become the very best versions of themselves. As I grow, I continue to add to it and refine it.

. . . .

The determination and focus required to live in The Zone may require sacrifices at times—it certainly has its costs.

However, any downside to being "different" and pursuing your mojo pales into insignificance compared to the costs and consequences of not doing so.

Consider heroes like Sir John Wilson who, having lost his sight in a school chemistry lab experiment, went on to lead *Sightsavers International*. In losing his sight, he gained a vision. He proved, dramatically, that it's not what happens to us that determines our lives—it's our attitude and what we do with what happens to us. Sir John said of himself that he was "lucky." He took an active part in that luck, though. He mastered a combination of attitude and behavior that led to opportunities that gave him the breaks and the confidence to get in The Zone and to have his own personal BREAKTHROUGH.

Being the best version of ourselves means having the attitude that, no matter what, we will find a career that will let us operate in The Zone.

If you aim for your "Zone," your life will rocket to a whole new altitude.

Experiencing the feelings of authenticity, freedom, liberation and joy of operating in The Zone are reward enough for me. Achieving a desired BREAKTHROUGH when you are there just puts a cherry on the icing on the cupcake!

Know Your Tribe

Being in The Zone energizes me—I feel ALIVE—and the more I am connected to my own power pack and energy supply, the more connected I feel to others.

I can't be the best version of myself in a swarm, but I can with my tribe—with those in my circle of influence who are my friends, my clients, anyone with whom I grow and learn, the people in my larger network—and most important, those individuals who mentor me.

My tribe helps me maintain a compelling vision in the face of vicious opposition and resistance. I get perspective from them and the energy to source "new" and original solutions to issues that others often see as major roadblocks.

The energy I received from my tribe helped me walk away from a life in which I would have survived, but never thrived. It's helped me have the courage to follow the path that leads me to being the best version of my Self—a path suited to my specific needs and areas for growth.

The more connected I am to my tribe, the better I become as a mentor–and as that best version of myself, the more I feel I can contribute to others.

I believe that we owe it to ourselves to find a career that allows us to operate in our Zone–and that it's our obligation to model this way of being for our family, community, country and humanity.

The only way we can inspire change in others is by being the change in ourselves first.

As Michelangelo wisely observed:

> **"The greatest danger for most of us is not that we aim too high and we miss It, rather that it is too low and we reach it."**

We are on a disaster course unless something significant changes. To avert the myriad scenarios that could potentially spell the end of humanity within the next 100 years, each of us, individually, needs to remain in our Zone–and continue to aim higher.

This BREAKTHROUGH equips us to work together to bring about the collective changes necessary to ensure that humanity has a bright future.

Breakthrough #16

Setting Your "Wheel of Life" in Motion

What happens to our Spirit as it encounters the events and circumstances of the "real" world? The very fact of being in a body, here on planet Earth, means that we will sometimes encounter situations that are difficult or traumatic. How we cope with that, how we overcome some disastrous experience and let our overcoming of it resonate magnificently within us, is a major part of how we grow and develop strength and wisdom as human beings.

The more "present" and receptive we are in the World, and the more coherent we are in all aspects of our life, the more we are in Flow. And being in Flow, or in The Zone, as the very best version of our Self with WavePower in action, we are likely to attract fewer difficult experiences. We are also likely to have greater access to the WillPower and WayPower to handle anything that Life brings.

Life happens. Suffering is optional . . . and so is HAPPINESS.

The ability to unleash and extract BREAKTHROUGH potential from what may appear, on the face of it, to be perfectly terrible experiences in life, is a profoundly spiritual undertaking.

I choose to believe that no matter what life throws at me, my Spirit will–perhaps after an inevitable period of confusion or suffering–embrace that experience and grow stronger as a result of it.

Or, as Winston Churchill said:

"When you're going through hell, keep going."

During a hellish time you may wind up thinking that it will never end, but it will. And when it does, you'll be all the stronger, spiritually and emotionally, from the challenging experience you've gone through.

Although we may never be able to truly know or "control" our ultimate Destiny, it certainly helps if we have a PLAN for our Life in the meantime. It's my belief that making a plan, even if we keep changing it along the way, also shapes our Destiny in each and every moment.

Now that we've explored each of the Spokes on the Wheel of Life in the context of various BREAKTHROUGHs, let's link them all together.

Being Your Own Spokesperson

When I developed the Wheel of Life model, it was for the purpose of helping me focus and identify my goals in these six key areas, or Spokes of my life:

Professional

Personal

Mental

Physical

Spiritual

Emotional

Another reason for creating this Tool is that I am a great believer in writing things down (even if electronically)—especially when it comes to what I want to achieve in the future. It's applying the same principle, or Universal Law, that we used in the Goals Posters in BREAKTHROUGH #3, except this time we're using words rather than images (although, there's nothing to stop you using both words and images in your Goals Poster or your Spokes!). In both exercises, we are "externalizing" our goals—and by externalizing them we "put them out there." And in doing so, we attract and manifest them.

Different Spokes for "Making : A : Difference" Folks

In this exercise, I take each of the Spokes on the Wheel of Life and map it separately using smaller wheels like cogs around the central wheel. Each of the smaller wheels/cogs supports and energizes my Wheel of Life.

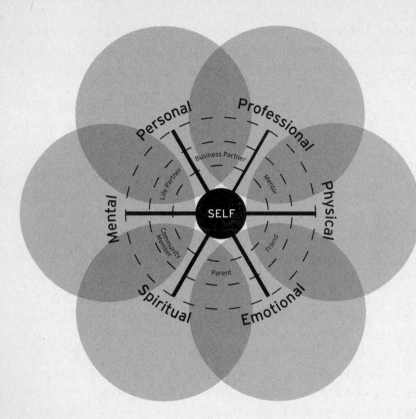

Radiating my "Very Best Version of Self"

I begin this exercise by focusing on my purpose . . .

I AM the very best version of my Self, at all times and in all ways.

I then list the various ROLES that I hold in my life in the center of the circle; e.g., Life Partner, Friend, Parent, Business Partner, Business Owner, Mentor, Community Member, Global Citizen, etc.

In the circle extending from each Spoke, I focus on and list the specific things in that particular area that will help me to become the very best version of myself.

This may also involve thinking about my values and how those values apply within each of the roles listed and the relationships or stakeholders I have within each of those roles.

I focus on the level of commitment that I have to each role and each thing I've listed.

It also becomes clear whether any section of the wheel dominates, or if a section is missing or out of balance in some other way—and I then explore how that might be impacting my life.

Representing my goals in this way allows me to see clearly what it is that makes me feel great, what excites me and what makes my heart hum. Seeing how each of the smaller wheels radiates energy back into my Wheel of Life (and vice versa) also allows me to "fine-tune" them.

Armed with this information, my FEELINGS become an internal NAVIGATION SYSTEM that helps guide me in moving toward those things in life that keep my Spokes, and hence my Wheel of Life, balanced—and to move away from anything that doesn't.

A Well-(in)Tensioned Wheel

In any wire wheel, Spokes need to have the right amount of TENSION to be flexible and strong enough to get you across any bumps in the road.

The next step in this exercise uses our INTENTION to increase the amount of "tension" or energy for each thing we DECIDED to list within the wheel attached to each Spoke.

In a two-column list, I expand on the information in the six smaller wheels and begin to think about my NEEDS—and what ACTIONS might fulfill those Needs in the context of my purpose; i.e., moving toward that "best version of Self."

There may be many Actions that could fulfill those Needs—and someone else with the same or a similar Need may choose completely different Actions to you. The Actions list may grow or change over time as you think of new and better ways to meet your core Needs.

Since we give energy to whatever it is that we focus on, I am very clear to list only Needs that would give me pleasure, and Actions that support me in moving toward what gives me pleasure, rather than anything I wish to avoid in life.

Here are some examples from my own workbook . . .

PROFESSIONAL

NEEDS	ACTIONS

• Meaning and purpose in my career
• Operate "in The Zone"
• Have a M : A : D network
• Have a M : A : D reputation
• Mastery of my craft
• Clients who value my skills and Making : A : Difference
	• Build and maintain a sustainable and profitable practice as The Mentor
	• Attract and work with my ideal clients (i.e., M : A : D leaders)
	• Build and maintain brand Me through:
	  • Being best in my chosen field
	  • Walking my talk
	  • Living M : A : D (ly)
	  • Delivering the "M : A : D Interview Series"
	  • Marketing & PR
	  • Social Networking—Website, Facebook, Twitter, etc.
	• Build The Rocket Club—the leading private invitation-only network comprising the next generation of business leaders, who are deeply interested in developing a profound understanding of consciousness, wisdom, and the essential truths of the arts, literature, philosophy, science, Quantum physics, health and ecology and integrating this knowledge in business for the betterment of the World
	• Fund the ongoing development of the DCMCWisdomWiki and have it become self-sustaining

PERSONAL

NEEDS	ACTIONS
• Be a great dad and support my children	• Regular quality time with my children and to "be there" for them
• Fun	• Check off the items on my Bucket List
• Self-managing	
• Self-motivated	• Create time for and enjoy my hobbies and interests
• Independence	
• To "Make A Difference"	• Be cash-flow positive (flow)
• Financial independence and stability	• Have surplus cash-flow (overflow) for philanthropy
• Authentic Self = Brand Me	• Create long-term financial security e.g., property, savings, investments

MENTAL

NEEDS	ACTIONS
• An ongoing, nourishing mental "menu" to expand my mind	• Continue to read wisdom writings
• Opportunities to express my creativity	• Write (this) my first book–and who knows? Perhaps a second!
• Exploration and development of new concepts and ideas	• Attract M : A : D individuals for the "M : A : D Interview Series"
• Discernment	• Attend seminars and workshops that expand my knowledge and my network
• Deeper understanding and insight (e.g., my friends)	
• Have my own Wisdom Council	• Bring to life the DCMCWisdomWiki

PHYSICAL

NEEDS	ACTIONS
• A healthy body • A nurturing environment • Being well organized / efficient • Simplicity • Orderliness	• Dally exercise • A balanced diet of healthy food • Quality sleep • Annual dental and medical checkups

SPIRITUAL

NEEDS	ACTIONS
• Alignment with my highest potential, purpose, values, Self • "Make myself useful" to others • Generosity	• Regular periods of silence, reflection and solitude • A simple life • Gratitude • Enjoy the journey • Celebrate successes

EMOTIONAL

NEEDS	ACTIONS
• Self-love • Being loving toward others • Being loved by others	• Live the principles in *The Invitation* (poem) • Only be in relationships that align with my relationship vision and values (see Heart diagram p. 139) • Live The Platinum Rule and see through the eyes of the other • Be forgiving and compassionate • Continue to work with my three "J"s on my own personal mastery

What are your NEEDS—and what ACTIONS would best support your needs?

You can achieve clarity around the six Spokes in your Wheel of Life by using TOOL #13 in the BREAKTHROUGH RETREAT WORKBOOK.

Executing any one of the Action items in each of your six lists constitutes A BREAKTHROUGH. It feels great to check them off!

I review my Spoke Lists of Needs and Actions regularly and add to or refine them as appropriate. And each time I do this exercise, I then update my Bucket List . . .

BUCKET LIST

Each of the six Spokes on my Wheel of Life functions like a filter to help me figure out what goes onto my **Bucket List**. Technically speaking, the term Bucket List came from the term "to kick the bucket," and so it's the list of things that we want to be, do or have—to accomplish and experience—before we die.

But there's no reason we can't have a new "Bucket" for every decade of our life, or even every year—and simply keep adding to it as we check things off the list. Use the "Bucket" metaphor in whatever way works for you—it's your "Bucket."

In the Hollywood movie of the same name, Jack Nicholson and Morgan Freeman set out making a Bucket List of things they wanted to accomplish to feel "complete" before they died. What started out as a list of things to do, and people and places to see, began to transform along the way—and transformed them, and others, in the process. Ultimately they discovered what gave real meaning and purpose to their lives—and that true healing came from love, acceptance, forgiveness—and feeling truly grateful!!!

Just one thing to note—anytime something on your Bucket List doesn't leave you feeling FABULOUS, or you find yourself questioning, "Is this all there is . . . ?" or "So what next . . . ?" and being unable to enjoy your achievements, please PAY ATTENTION.

It's a sure sign that it's time to go back and review your Spokes, to reassess your true Needs—and the Actions that support those needs.

What's on your Bucket List?

When there's absolute clarity around what's truly important to you, you will not only make things happen—your Bucket can empty (by checking things off the list!) as fast as you fill it.

And every time you check another Action off your list, you are positively reinforcing and energizing your ability to live as the very best version of your Self.

So set your Wheels in motion, load up that Bucket . . . and enjoy the ride.

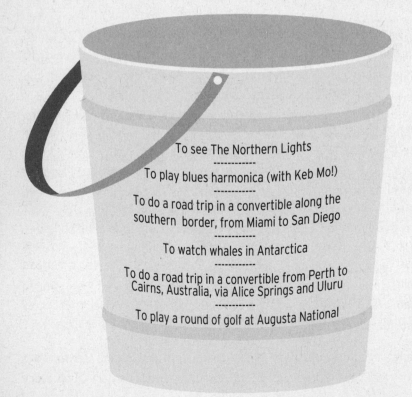

To see The Northern Lights

To play blues harmonica (with Keb Mo!)

To do a road trip in a convertible along the southern border, from Miami to San Diego

----

To watch whales in Antarctica

To do a road trip in a convertible from Perth to Cairns, Australia, via Alice Springs and Uluru

----

To play a round of golf at Augusta National

Breakthrough #17

Failure Isn't Falling Down . . . It's Staying Down

I love to read or listen to motivational and inspirational stories like that of Sylvester Stallone and the movie, *Rocky*. It reminds me that no matter what circumstances we find ourselves in, there is always a way to make a BREAKTHROUGH if we are determined.

Like so many "great" stories, there are differing versions, especially on the Internet, so I have no idea how much of this one is actually true. Perhaps one day I can ask Sylvester Stallone? In the meantime, whether or not all the details are *exactly* as things occurred for him, I've been inspired and motivated by his *Rocky* journey. So here's my version . . .

Sylvester Stallone grew up in suburban Pennsylvania, where he first started acting. He then spent two years teaching at the American College of Switzerland in Geneva. After arriving back in the United States, he became a drama student at the University of Miami, where he also started to write.

He left full-time education before graduating and moved to New York City to pursue his dream of acting. He auditioned for pretty much every casting agent in NYC, with absolutely no success. He decided to spend more time writing while waiting for his big break.

In 1974 he was cast as one of the leads in *The Lords of Flatbush*. He also received his first writing credit for additional dialogue on the same film. Despite this break, he struggled to sustain momentum in his career. He kept auditioning and received one rejection after the next. He continued to write more screenplays and each pitch led to yet another rejection.

He could barely feed his family. Then one day, walking through NYC, he wandered into a library to warm himself up. This became a regular habit during the winter months. During his visits to the library he began reading books written by great writers. This gave him an extra edge in his own endeavors and he pursued these more and more.

By this stage he was desperate to get work, but wouldn't take any old job, as he had his dream. He wanted to be an actor. For him it was only a matter of "when" not "if." Along the way, he had to resort to many regrettable things, including pawning his wife's jewelry.

He was so broke by this time that he decided he had to sell his best friend, his dog—as he could no longer afford to feed him. Stallone waited outside a local liquor store asking people if they would buy his dog. He wanted $50, but eventually someone negotiated with him and bought it for around $25. He was devastated at having to do this.

Two weeks later he was sitting at home watching a boxing match on TV. Chuck Wepner, the underdog, was getting absolutely whooped by Muhammad Ali, but somehow, against the odds, kept holding his ground and coming back for more. The underdog was really fighting to win, despite the slim chance he would ever even get close to it.

The example set by this fighter inspired Stallone to begin writing a story whose main character exhibited similar heroic traits. For more than 20 hours, he wrote nonstop—the entire script for *Rocky*.

He began trying to sell the screenplay to many producers, meeting with the same dispiriting process of endless rejections. This went on for months.

Yet still he kept sending out the script that he had written. Eventually someone loved it and agreed to make the film. Stallone told this person that he wanted to play the part of Rocky. The studio declined and told him he was a writer, not an actor. He disagreed and said he was an actor first. Despite his poverty, he turned down the offer of more than $100,000 for the movie rights.

A couple of weeks later the studio contacted him with an even higher offer—and Stallone still insisted that he should play Rocky. Once again, the studio turned him down. Was he crazy?

The money on offer kept escalating—he was offered a quarter of a million dollars *not* to play the lead role in his own movie. The price eventually rose to around $325,000—and still he held out. He was certain that he was Rocky. He could feel every ounce of Rocky's pain and determination. He wouldn't need to "act"! There would be no compromise.

Eventually the studio offered him just $35,000—and the lead role. Sylvester Stallone accepted.

The first thing he did was go back to the liquor store to buy back his dog. He waited three days for the guy to come by, and finally there he was with the dog. Stallone offered the guy $100 to buy back the dog, but the man declined. Despite increasing his offer, the man continued to refuse it—once again Stallone kept pursuing his goal. It ended up costing him $15,000 and a part in the movie to buy back his dog. Both the guy and the dog are actually in *Rocky*.

Of course we all know what happened next. The movie won the Oscar for Best Picture at the Academy Awards in 1977.

Stallone had kept all the rejection letters and written down all the things said by those he'd approached—those who had said no one would ever want to watch the film. Stallone read them all the night he won the Academy Award. Years of rejection and negativity had been transformed into something supremely positive—an inspirational movie loved by many—and this Oscar was proof.

This wonderful story shows that we have inside ourselves all the resources we will ever need to overcome any obstacle and achieve any aim we have in life, no matter what our age, background, color or gender.

True persistence pays off every time, in every circumstance. Persistence will fight off failure faster than skill or luck ever could. Just ask Sylvester Stallone. He knew his outcome, persisted . . . and achieved it to live his dream.

What would YOU fight *that* hard for?

What would YOU hock your dog for?

What would YOU *never* compromise over?

This segues neatly into my all-time favorite film clip. It's the legendary scene in *The Empire Strikes Back* when Luke Skywalker goes off in search of the Jedi Master, Yoda, to be taught about "The Force."

Luke, of course, has imagined a great warrior as his mentor and teacher and is somewhat underwhelmed when he finally has to accept that this funny little creature is in fact Yoda, the Jedi Master.

There are just so many amazing lines in the film, but I used to make my kids watch this particular scene over and over again.

The punch line comes at the end of the scene. Luke has only managed to raise the rocket halfway out of the swamp before giving up—and Yoda then lifts it out entirely, using only "The Force."

When Luke says, **"I don't believe it!"** Yoda responds with the immortal words, **"And that is why you fail."**

And that is also why WE fail! We TRY! And we give up too easily.

What do you need to change to rocket out of your "swamp"—to make a BREAKTHROUGH?

Do You Have Rock(y)s in Your Head?

Almost every great leader has at some point "fallen over." For example, the founder of Starbucks was turned down more than 300 times before he received funding, and Walt Disney more than 200 times.

My mom once said to me that she much admired my ability to overcome setbacks, to pick myself up, dust myself off and get back in the saddle and ride on to the next adventure.

After the demise of my second, and very short, "rebound" marriage, my mom made the same comment to me once again. That was a turning point in my life.

As much as I appreciated her acknowledgment of my stamina, perseverance and self-belief, I (along with a few friends!) questioned whether I had a case of the proverbial "rocks in my head"–at least when it came to choosing marriage partners.

In that moment, I decided that a much better strategy would be to avoid falling over quite so often in the first place–and that learning to be more discerning might prevent me from making many of the mistakes that caused me to fall over. Rather than take a "reactive" stance, like deciding to never get married again, I chose to be "proactive" and do things very differently in choosing my next partner.

I equally applied this distinction of adding "discernment" to my determination in my career.

That conversation with my mom was a "wake up" call–it was the **inflection point** that catalyzed the journey of personal mastery and consciousness that I continue to be on to this day.

Clearly, after reading other stories about my personal adventures in BREAKTHROUGH, I'm not claiming that I haven't occasionally fallen over every now and again since.

But I've always found a way to get back up!

And so can you . . . right NOW!

. . . .

Whether you've been reading the chapters of BREAKTHROUGH in sequence or randomly, now is a good time to press the PAUSE button.

It's time to take a REALITY CHECK on your approach—and to gauge whether you're in alignment with what you set out to achieve when you started.

Keeping in mind what you want to achieve right now . . . please think about how you've approached reading and/or working through this book.

- Have you just zoomed through and only "read" the questions—or have you stopped and been actually answering them and using the TOOLs along the way?

- Where in the book or process did you get stuck? Where did you give up? Where did you think "I'll come back to this"—and did you?

- Where did you think, "I need help?" Did you ask for it? Who did you ask? Did you get it? And if not, why not?

- And, do any of the previous behaviors describe what you do in your life? Is this how you approach life?

Most people, once they have their Vision, find they have the WillPower—but they don't realize exactly what's needed in terms of resources (i.e., the WayPower) or know how to get what they need.

They don't understand the practical steps required to execute their brilliant idea—or if they do, they don't effectively communicate and enroll others in their vision. They have unrealistic expectations of others' level of interest, understanding, buy-in, and hence, their commitment.

They often have no comprehension of the time these steps take to implement—especially in large global organizations. Many times in my work I've encountered the classic scenario where a CEO dreams up a "genius idea" that needs to be rolled out globally. When the CEO visits the China office six months later, he or she can't understand why it hasn't been implemented—because the CEO's brain is already three brilliant visions further down the track!

Having the right mentor can make the difference here by joining the dots between the CEO's brilliant idea and the ability of the organization or team or stakeholders to deliver on their vision.

Often, after clients have shared their brilliant new ideas or products or services or initiatives, I've said, "Now is a good time to take a well-earned two-week vacation." They protest, of course, that now would be precisely the wrong time to take a vacation, having presented the world with their amazing vision. My job is to convince them that the rest of their top team—who all love the idea, too, and are feeling inspired—will now need some time to figure out how to integrate and implement this vision.

I have seen far too many great ideas abandoned by the roadside as people's impatience and expectation of instant "results" gave way to lethargy and boredom once they realized there was no "quick fix" and they had to get real about the time and effort required to roll out the changes necessary for their idea to succeed.

Although we think of companies like Google and Facebook and Twitter as huge overnight successes, so many of these "instant success" businesses actually had several years of doing the hard work (the 10,000 hours)—with their founders doing for the business what Sylvester Stallone did to launch *Rocky.*

These companies and the Sly Stallones are the rare few who "make it"—whose rockets actually take off! How many other great businesses—and visions—never leave the gantry, but might have succeeded if they'd had a mentor to help them achieve those critical BREAKTHROUGHs?

And how much faster, or more easily, might those who actually did launch and succeed have "made it" with a mentor by their side?

My advice is to take a moment to ask yourself:

> What have I learned in BREAKTHROUGH that I already knew, but am not doing? And why?

> What have I learned that I now want to do? And what's needed to make sure it happens?

Commit to being the best version of yourself and choose just one of the BREAKTHROUGH ideas—any one you like—and figure out what you need to do to take it from "idea" to "delivery." Do the TOOLs. And find a friend or a mentor who will work with you and hold you accountable.

If you're still reading this, but thinking you don't actually need to DO anything to get a BREAKTHROUGH, hopefully it's because this book resonates with you and you've enjoyed a few "feel good" moments along the way. But If I haven't yet convinced you to take that five-degree (5º) course correction, my job is not yet done.

If BREAKTHROUGH is destined for that pile of books you've read that contains great ideas, but you have not yet done anything about them . . . then maybe it's time for me to push a few buttons.

I apologize in advance if what I am about to say offends . . . but it has to be said.

Just because you're reading this, it doesn't mean that the magic contained in its pages will somehow magically rub off on you like pixie dust.

Unless you take a "never quit," "no exits," "Rocky's Road" approach—you probably won't achieve too many of these BREAKTHROUGHs in your life. Or they won't be sustainable.

And what will come up is your old defensive behaviors and justifications.

You'll blame the circumstances of your life.

You'll decide that the BREAKTHROUGHs in this book don't work.

Or that having a mentor can't add any value to your life.

And . . . that you can't "Make : A : Difference."

If you recognize any of this in yourself, or your buttons have been pushed right now, I've done my job. Just like my mom did for me when she inadvertently reminded me how often I was falling down. Ouch!

You now have a choice.

You can recognize how you make yourself "fall over"–how you sabotage yourself. And you can stop and decide to learn to do something different.

Remember, falling over is not failing–it's simply a learning opportunity.

There are two "L"s in "falling–they stand for "Living" and "Learning" (more on that in BREAKTHROUGH #19).

Failing, on the other hand, has only one "L"–there's no "Learning" when you believe you've failed.

When you "get up"–rather than "give up"–you become a stronger, even better version of your Self.

Always be–and do–your best. Even if your "best" means taking time out for a while to adjust your Spokes and regroup.

Whatever happens, get back on your bike!

Who needs dragons to slay when there are endless undreamed of M : A : D (ad)ventures to be had?

Breakthrough #18

The Consciousness Connection . . . Joining the Dots

How many more wise men, sages, gurus and rock stars need to tell us that WE ARE ALL ONE, before we join the dots and truly "get" that everything we think, say and do affects everything and everyone everywhere?

If only we were clever enough to find a way to measure CONSCIOUSNESS on a massive scale. I can certainly count the ways in which the lack of conscious awareness of our connectedness impacts on my life—and on our planet.

Consciousness is a word that's been used in many different ways. A bit like that tired old joke about pornography, which has often been applied to leadership: it's hard to define, but you know it when you see it.

That's why I prefer to speak about CONNECTEDNESS, or in other words, being CONSCIOUS of our INTERCONNECTION. I define this as:

The ability to see, feel, appreciate, acknowledge and factor into solutions that "interconnection" exists between ALL things— and combine this with a level of self-awareness, knowledge and discernment about doing the right things in the right way for the benefit of the whole.

I wonder how many of the following statements about consciousness and our connectedness you resonate with?

1. If everyone in the world were more aware and conscious of the fact that everything is connected, there would be far less war, poverty, crime, disease and hunger.

2. Babies innately know how to bond and connect. Not one baby ever born knew naturally how to hate. Not one baby ever born knew anything other than unconditional love for other sentient beings. We taught them to think that others are "different," that we are not connected.

3. The global population explosion is unsustainable. If we fail to see the connection between unchecked population growth and our impact on the Earth and her resources, it will lead to increased poverty, disease, famine, hunger, crime and war.

4. If we continue with the current lack of awareness around our connectedness, there is a greater than 50 percent chance we will wipe out all human existence within a few hundred years.

5. Economic systems drive world politics, creating divisiveness and fueling war and unrest. Religion also fails to generate sufficient

consciousness around our connectedness to create world peace and harmony.

6. Our economic models cause businesses to act for "short-term gain" (survival), rather than make the conscious "long-term" decisions required for humanity to thrive. Failure to acknowledge our connection with the Earth, and one another, leads to large-scale pollution and man-made disasters that accelerate the potential for the destruction of humanity.

7. The growth of any business, organization or nation can never be greater than the level of consciousness of its leader; i.e., that leader's connection with the people, and his or her awareness of connectedness with the community, and the planet.

8. If World leaders and business leaders were as "connected" as Gandhi, Mandela, Wilberforce and Mother Teresa, we would be less likely to cause harm to others, to harm Mother Nature and to ultimately destroy ourselves.

9. Just as lack of connectedness is something that is learned, we can learn to become more aware and regain our sense of connection.

10. Intuitively, I know that a piece of the solution lives inside ME—it's not something I have to find "out there." I know the journey starts within me . . . and that YOU are also connected in this.

We all innately KNOW that we are connected, and yet we act as if we believe we are alone and powerless. We become overwhelmed by what appears to be the futility of our efforts, amidst what can feel, at times, like a tsunami of unconsciousness.

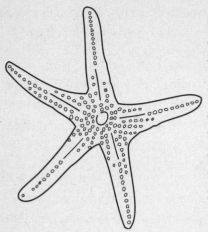

If we feel isolated and that our efforts are futile, it's because we, too, have gone unconscious.

We are identifying with those apocryphal starfish stranded on the beach, waiting for someone else to come and rescue us—rather than identifying with the boy taking action by throwing the starfish back into the ocean.

We've forgotten who we ARE and the "difference" we are capable of making. As Mother Teresa once said:

"If we have no peace, it is because we have forgotten we belong to each other."

How intelligent is it to believe—and to behave as if—we are not connected?

In my teens and twenties, "intelligence" was all about IQ (Intelligence Quotient)—or the capacity of our intellect. To get ahead, we were told, we needed to go to college and eventually to business school to get an MBA.

I think that there's now universal agreement that the MBA model for business has inflicted vast harm. We've created a scenario where a select handful of elite, rich and powerful "leaders" hold the majority of the world's wealth. This "intelligence" has been used to achieve "control" and to "power over" everything from Nature to nations, not to mention the generations of schoolchildren who were labeled and limited for life by learning they had a "low" IQ score.

Once we started to figure out that IQ wasn't enough, we searched for answers and found we needed to improve the way we worked together. It was all about understanding one another better and collaborating more effectively.

Welcome EQ (Emotional Quotient)—our ability to understand our impact on others and their impact on us! We all quickly learned that we were dysfunctional, greedy, selfish, and disinterested in the greater good. We cleverly applied this new intelligence to manipulate others and give ourselves a competitive advantage—and it turns out those with the wealth had already been using the "secret" of EQ for centuries.

We became disillusioned with "people" and so turned to "The Universe" for answers. Of course! What was missing was SQ (Spiritual Quotient)—the capacity to connect with the Infinite and access a Source of wisdom greater than ourselves. While the theory and research is great, interestingly, the majority of business leaders still resist using words like "spiritual," "consciousness"—and yes, even "love"—in the workplace! Perhaps that's a legacy of the hordes of New Age consultants who descended on the corporate world armed with EQ and SQ, yet were completely ungrounded in the realities of business.

Somehow none of these "intelligences" have really worked. Why? Because we have always sought the solution to the problems we are trying to solve outside ourselves. It's "them" over there! If only "they" would do something different. We can all see that what "they" are doing isn't working and/or won't be sustainable. But what do we do about it?

What's missing is CQ–**CONNECTION QUOTIENT**–the capacity to consciously recognize and factor in the connectedness of all things.

This intelligence brings with it the realization that it's impossible to "get away" with anything–or from anyone, or to anywhere–and that whenever we try to do so, there's a cost or consequence.

Ironically, it's never from others, or our past, or our environment that we are really trying to "get away." The problem is not "out there."

It resides "in here"–it's how we FEEL on the inside about those things that we are trying to get away from on the outside–but there is no escaping from ourselves.

The good news, then, is that the SOLUTION must, therefore, also reside within us.

We simply need to stop "getting away" from connecting within–to stop "getting away with" disconnecting from our core authentic Self.

It's an inside job.

The Courage to Lead Through Love

Being a great leader of others demands consciously connecting with others.

However, before we can authentically connect with others, we must connect with and fully accept our Self.

"Connecting within" can be even more scary than connecting with others—it's much easier to pretend with others.

Being authentic and real requires us to "own" our beliefs, fears, emotions, limitations and vulnerabilities.

The upside of connecting within, being real with ourselves and accepting ourselves fully is **Self-Leadership**, which arises from the connection between our own hearts and souls and minds.

When we master connecting within, we become aware of the interconnection between all things. And then, we cannot help but do the right things—for the right reasons—and do them the right way.

Achieving the BREAKTHROUGH of Self-Leadership is a crucial stepping-stone on the path toward being a great leader of others.

Conscious connection with others requires a willingness to authentically share our real selves. To show up and be fully alive and present, to be vulnerable, intimate, genuine, and emotionally and spiritually available. To move beyond our current beliefs, fears, limitations—and take decisive action.

It also requires honesty, truthfulness, integrity, and courage—the courage to go beyond our current boundaries.

Courage is not the absence of fear. It's what we do when we feel fear. It takes courage to risk making a fool of yourself. Wherever you find success, follow the story back—you will always find it started off with courage somewhere. Courage is the beginning of all greatness.

Dr. Martin Luther King Jr., whose M : A : D contribution was to envision a world without prejudice, where disconnection between people no longer existed, said:

> "Cowardice asks the question—is it safe? Expediency asks the question—is it politic? Vanity asks the question—is it popular? But conscience asks the question—is it right? And there comes a time when one must take a position that is neither safe, nor politic, nor popular; but one must take it because it is right."

Conscious leaders touch our hearts and inspire and motivate us because they are connected within themselves. They trust that inner voice enough to say, "This just might work, so let's give it a go."

When we encounter authentic leaders who display compassion, love, courage and GRACE, they give us permission to do the same—to open our hearts and connect with and embrace the qualities we see in them within ourselves.

If, like the Cowardly Lion in *The Wizard of Oz*, you cannot "own" your courage, you might as well give up now. Without being connected to your courage as a foundation, the BREAKTHROUGHs contained in the following chapters are unsustainable.

Before you give up, though, I suggest you revisit BREAKTHROUGH #12 and apply the same strategy my dad suggested when I needed to learn to be more "gentlemanly-like":

> If you are not courageous or brave, the bravest thing to do is to pretend you are—and act accordingly.

The World would be a much better place if we loved ourselves and others unconditionally, connected deeply and had the courage to tell one another the truth.

It takes courage to be a loving person—and to tell others we love them.

My own father never told me he loved me. The nearest he ever got was when I once told him I loved him—and he replied, "ditto."

This hole in my soul caused me years and years of pain. It drove many unhelpful behaviors in me. It drove my need for accomplishment and achievement and recognition and appreciation and acceptance, more than anything and everything else.

Only when I finally forgave him—and myself—and accepted him for who he is, did I finally realize that my father had loved me to the best of his abilities. I came to understand that his "Love Language" was his actions and deeds—well, most of them!

Healing and releasing my pain meant it would no longer drive repeated dysfunctional behaviors—and integrating the new learning from my earlier experiences opened up new possibilities in relating.

If I had a dollar for every man who's told me that his dad never told him he loved him, I could have retired a long time ago. I see a direct link between this perceived lack of love and the inability to communicate it—and the acting out of dysfunctional behaviors by many leaders in areas from business and politics to religious institutions.

For the successful leaders whom I most admire and aspire to be like, **love is a way of life**. They just "do" love in everything they touch. They believe in the essential goodness of people.

They understand that consciousness means recognizing the connectedness between all things. And that it must start within themselves in connecting up and balancing their Physical, Mental, Spiritual, Emotional, Professional and Personal Spokes. They understand that their life is only ever going to be as aligned "out there" as it is on the "inside."

Harnessing Interconnectedness

One way that conscious connection expresses in the World is through "being of service."

> After the verb "love," surely the most important verb is "serve."

Deeply listening to another is being of "service" (remember MVE?). So is "being interested" more than "being interesting." And following the Platinum Rule. (All of these are in BREAKTHROUGH #12.)

Success in life has very little to do with what we gain for ourselves, and much more to do with what we give back to, and enable, in others. Connecting with others in this way is the very purpose of life–it's not just "something to do in our spare time."

Giving service to others is the price of admission to a meaningful life.

When we embrace the idea that we are all connected, we connect with and inspire others' hearts in ways that help both parties become the very best versions of themselves.

If we know that it's important to raise awareness in people and harness the power of human consciousness, why do we have no way of quantifying it?

I wish I were clever enough to devise a curriculum for creating conscious connection, a college or university degree program—and to measure its positive benefits. Clearly at the level of nations, measuring revenues and profits and cash flow, GDP, EBITDA and EPS is not working.

In assessing people, why do personality profiles focus predominantly on "left-brain" competencies rather than "soft skills" required for relating and connecting? We need to be able to measure both, because it's both parts of us—and the connection between them—that we need to grow and develop and nurture if we want to achieve the joy of conscious connection, which in turn enables us to become the very best versions of ourselves.

As John Lennon sang in *Imagine*, "one day the world will live as one."

We are already connected—we ARE all ONE. We just need to start behaving that way.

Or, as missionary and Nobel Peace Prize winner, Albert Schweitzer said:

> **"Just as the wave cannot exist for itself, but is ever a part of the heaving surface of the ocean, so must I never live my life for itself, but always in the experience which is going on around me."**

And just as WE are not separate, neither do these 20 BREAKTHROUGH ideas exist in isolation.

It's not because things are difficult that we sometimes do not dare. It's because we do not dare that things are difficult.

In daring to connect and step up with this BREAKTHROUGH . . .

Our role as a **LEADER OF SELF** is to connect within, to be an integrated, authentic Self that is aligned Personally and Professionally, as well as in our Mental, Physical, Spiritual and Emotional Spokes. Our internal alignment attracts authentic relationships that help us become the best versions of ourselves, and vice versa. Being the best versions of ourselves is how we best serve others–and also lead others.

Our role as a **LEADER OF OTHERS** is to connect and inspire one another to find and optimize the greatness in all of us.

Achieving and consciously living in awareness of our connectedness isn't easy.

It means taking responsibility for whatever shows up in our life.

But is there any other choice?

Breakthrough #19

R. U. "M : A : D"?
(Making : A : Difference)

What does the phrase, **"Make A Difference"** mean to you?

And why should you **"Make A Difference"**?

If you are completely fulfilled in your life—and happy with the way things are heading in our society—and the World—then this BREAKTHROUGH may not speak to you.

But since there's far more complaining than gratitude going on "out there," far more fear than love pervading our media and on the streets, and given that spiraling debt rather than wealth and abundance is the reality most individuals wake up to every morning (not to mention some of the world's most powerful nations!)—then perhaps you feel that something should or could be different.

It's not enough to just say that things "should be different," though—as if someone else is responsible for fixing them.

In the 18th century, Adam Smith, often regarded as the Father of Economics, wrote about the "invisible hand" of the market. Smith's writings reflected his profoundly religious and moral perspective. In other words, he felt a connection to something greater than himself. It's patently clear that "the market" has not simply fallen over—it is seriously failing. And it's our failure to perceive the "connection" between all things (including competing systems and agendas) that underlies this failure. If there is, or ever was, an "invisible hand" to reach out and rescue the whole system, we are no longer connected to it.

Whether it's "the market" or our life, there is no "it" or "they" to solve or fix this for us—we need to do it ourselves. It's up to us now.

If all we leave to the next generation is "the system" in its current form—and "money"—it will be like leaving behind poison. It's passing on to the next generation what hasn't worked for us—the "problems" we couldn't solve and just buried in that file labeled "Too Complicated to Sort Out Now."

Is this the legacy that our generation wants to be remembered for? This is insanity!

What we need to pass on is LOVE. And that journey starts with SELF. Learning to LOVE ourselves—raising our awareness—learning to love others—and learning to authentically CONNECT. We need to pass on the awareness that we are all connected.

It's my belief that if 51 percent of the population of the world did just one thing every day to "make a difference" to the life of someone else that they didn't know, the level of "connection" in the World would increase such that there would be no hunger, crime, poverty, war or disease within a matter of decades.

This kind of M : A : D—Making A Difference—is the only way to go.

The Melody of Life

Life has four "notes" or "parts," which I call the four "L"s. They are:

LEARNING

LOVING

LIVING . . . and

Leaving a LEGACY.

Together, they create the chords that form the "melody" of our life.

In life, most people start off LEARNING a lot, but stop after finishing their education, and their learning decreases rapidly as they get older.

The LOVING part starts in our twenties, but this, too, soon tapers off as responsibilities begin to take over from hormonal and biological drivers.

The third "note" of life, the LIVING part, is about manifesting our ambitions.

However, if these first three notes were all there ever was to your Life, how do you imagine you would feel at the end?

I believe that as you reflect back on your life, there would be a huge sense that something is missing—a sense of what "could have been." Unlived dreams give rise to a massive shortfall in fulfillment.

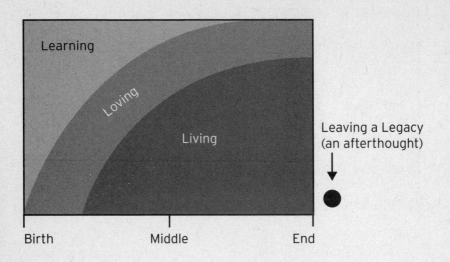

Learning

Loving

Living

Leaving a Legacy
(an afterthought)

Birth   Middle   End

What's missing is the fourth "note"—LEGACY, or what we leave behind—
and I'm not just talking about the kids' inheritance. This is the additional
resonant line of our "song" that adds richness, depth and harmony. It's
M : A : D—Making : A : Difference.

Complete happiness, joy and fulfillment can only be experienced if we
leave behind a Legacy that involves Making : A : Difference.

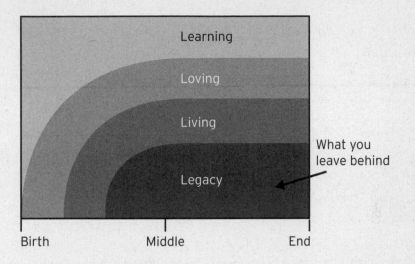

The four life "notes" need to look more like the second diagram for us to achieve Personal Mastery—our ultimate goal.

This fourth stage—Legacy—is the vital ingredient that makes *the* difference between living an ordinary life—and an *extra*-ordinary life.

By simply shifting the start and end times for each life part, we can increase or decrease the total area of any of the "L notes" and hence the impact that each particular "L" has in our life.

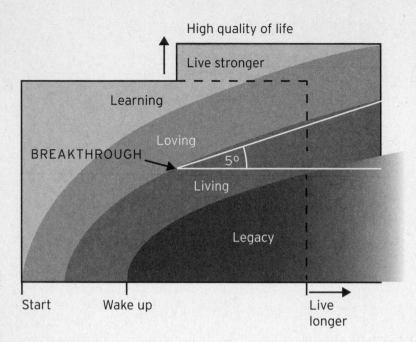

The shift that occurred when I "woke up" and realized that I wanted to achieve Personal Mastery and become the very best version of myself, is represented in the third diagram by both the increased area of Legacy—and the section that extends horizontally and vertically beyond the original boundary. I also became aware that it's possible to create and LEAVE a Legacy that continues after I die.

Prior to that, like so many people, I had been unconsciously drifting along, following the crowd and doing what was expected of me.

I've always loved this poem by Milton Berle:

> **I would rather be a could-be**
> **if I cannot be an are;**
> **Because a could-be is a maybe**
> **who is reaching for a star.**
> **I'd rather be a has-been**
> **than a might-have-been, by far;**
> **For a might-have-been, has never been,**
> **But a has was once an are.**

At the point when I chose to become the best version of myself (rather than simply a better version of myself), the QUALITY of my life immediately began to expand (the vertical expansion).

I know that this sounds unbelievably simple. However, having now seen this in my own life—and also replicated this experience with others, especially my clients—I know it to be true.

The day you commit to and take action toward becoming the best version of yourself will be the day the Quality of your life begins to expand.

The difference may be almost imperceptible on Day 1—or massive. And at times it may plateau (but if you take BREAKTHROUGH #17 on board, you won't stay stuck for long!). The wonderful thing is that the effects are cumulative and exponential.

The day you start "making a difference" to others will be the day your M : A : D **life inflection point** kicks in and you will move from living a good life to living a GREAT life.

Just keep depositing into your M : A : D investment account and it will generate lifelong dividends.

Embracing each of the BREAKTHROUGHs outlined in this book has not only significantly increased the QUALITY of my life. As I continue to "course-correct" within each one of them, I believe I'm also increasing the QUANTITY (length) of my life.

Implementing the specific BREAKTHROUGHs that resonate for you will do the same in your life.

Before we explore the "how to" and the benefits of M : A : D, let's look at each of the four "notes" in turn:

Learning

Wherever we're located in the world, whatever gender, race or religion we are, the first part of life for all of us is about LEARNING.

When we are born—some say from the moment of conception—we are like a sponge, absorbing information about our environment and the World.

Learning takes many forms as we grow, from learning by osmosis through to modeling our behaviors on what we observe in our family and peers, and also formal education, career education and personal or spiritual reflection. Ultimately this "note" is about trying to make sense of the extraordinarily diverse planet onto which we have landed.

We learn how we get things done around here, how we progress, who and what it is that we need to know to equip us to function in the world that we are expected to perform in.

To some extent, the process of learning continues with us for the rest of our lives. The day we stop learning is the day we start dying.

At some point in our Learning, life begins to layer in the next "note" as we learn about relating and connecting with others.

Loving

Love is a primary need, and as we saw in BREAKTHROUGH #11, it's one of the main "drivers" of our BREAKTHROUGHs, just as it can inspire them.

We learn in the LOVING "note" how to Love Others (remember the Platinum Rule?). And equally important, we must learn to Love Self, for without this, we cannot truly love another—whether that is our Beloved, our children, our friends, our tribe—or our family of origin. Only from a place of Self Love can we love others, including our enemies—recognizing that everything that is in them, also exists within us!

Few achieve this Love of Self in a healthy way. Society is filled with examples of how we seek to change the outside; i.e., change our appearance or our identity through what we HAVE, rather than changing the "inside"—who we ARE.

Loving is all about our relationship with our Self, our relationships with others—and "connection."

Living

While the Learning and Loving "notes" continue to sound through to the end of our lives (or at least we should want that they do), soon another "note" arises—LIVING.

We begin to see new possibilities and start to action our dreams—finding the right partner to love and share our lives with, enjoying the infinite blessing of becoming a parent, making a living doing something we are in The Zone with, living somewhere we really want to live and in a place that we love living, seeing the World and experiencing interests that broaden our horizons, pursuing goals that lift our spirits and so on.

This is the time that most people see as the **prime years** of their lives.

Legacy

Yet one day, perhaps somewhere between the ages of 40 and 70, we might "wake up" and begin to have thoughts like, "Well, I've learned so much, I have some great relationships, I'm happy with my life and it's all gone reasonably to plan . . . but actually, if my life were to end tomorrow, I wonder how I would feel? What am I leaving behind? And is it something I could be proud of?"

You start to think about what your LEGACY is going to be—at work, in your primary relationship, with your offspring, in your tribe—and in the World.

What, you wonder, do you want the people standing around your graveside to say about you?

What do you want your family, friends, the people who live in your community, your country or who you are connected with internationally, to be saying about you?

The feelings and thinking stimulated by this "note" can be a kind of "spiritual awakening."

The yearning to leave a Legacy manifests itself very differently from person to person—there is no "right" or "better"—it's a very personal choice. At the end you are answerable only to your SELF.

So the big question is whether, at the end of your life, you want to ensure that your LEGACY has made, and will make, a difference to others.

I am sure the answer is, "YES, of course!" especially when you contemplate the alternative scenario at your funeral, in which the holy man's eulogy is simply, "Let us reflect upon David's life and accept that, during his 80 years on this planet, he made absolutely no difference to anyone or anything!"

Legacy adds a richness that brings "harmony" to the dissonant cacophony of life.

It culminates in the "symphony" that you leave behind.

Leaving a Legacy—the M : A : D Way

How would you score yourself right now in terms of Making : A : Difference and leaving a LEGACY?

This BREAKTHROUGH is about setting things in motion now to leave behind something that is truly M : A : D (Making : A : Difference).

And, just like saving for your old age, it's never a bad time to start making deposits into your Legacy bank account!

One of my favorite M : A : D movies of all time is *Pay It Forward*. My big takeaway from the movie was that whenever anybody gives up, everybody loses. When I give up, everyone I love and care about loses.

Most people resist even starting to "make a difference" because they believe they are insignificant and that what's required of them in the World is too overwhelming. Although they may want to help, they don't know where or how to begin.

As Mother Teresa said:

"If you can't feed a hundred people, then just feed one."

In *Pay It Forward*, the idea was to feed three! So why not start off by simply making a difference to just one complete stranger? Even though you are only one person in the world, to that one person, you will mean the world!

I wish that I had understood when I was 20 years old how the four "L notes" would play out in my own life. I would have made some very different choices along the way.

I wish I'd understood that simple things like offering to take a photo for random strangers—with their camera—so they'd have a wonderful memory of their experience, Makes : A : Difference.

Or that genuinely asking a shop assistant, "How are you?" and truly listening to their response, Makes : A : Difference.

Making : A : Difference is a way of life and an attitude. It was a wise person who said, "If you have much, give your wealth. If you have little, give your heart!"

In the context of leaving a Legacy, Making : A : Difference means **making more discerning, more aware, and more LOVING decisions and choices.**

Acting on the decision to leave a Legacy can compel us to do things we would never otherwise do—like creating a unique organization, a lasting community or global initiative that never existed before, a legendary movie script like *Rocky* or a song or work of art that deeply moves people.

Whether it's been done before or is something completely new and fresh, the only thing that matters is that we are proud to be associated with it as our Legacy.

There's no set or "right" way to Make : A : Difference—or to create your Legacy—but when the two are linked, the impact can be exponential. Start with baby-steps and only build as big as feels right for you.

Your happiness and sense of fulfillment will expand in direct proportion to the effort and energy that you expend in Making : A : Difference. The more M : A : D you are, the greater the quality and quantity of your life.

So, the question to ask yourself right now is:

Am I M : A : D? Am I Making : A : Difference?

And if not, you can start right now by reflecting on these questions each evening as you go to sleep:

- What have I LEARNED today?

- How have I LOVED today?

- How have I LIVED today?

- How have I MADE A DIFFERENCE today?

. . . and then, decide to improve tomorrow.

When it's time to turn M : A : D into leaving a M : A : D Legacy, then ALSO ask . . .

- What DIFFERENCE can I make TODAY that will shape or impact TOMORROW—for myself and others?

- And what DIFFERENCE will that continue to make the day after (or even in years to come!)—for myself and others—whether or not I am here to see the outcome?

We are the stories we tell ourselves. So if we tell ourselves we can't make a difference . . . guess what? We won't ever begin.

But if we tell ourselves that we can and do make a difference to others—and that it can be lasting—we'll figure out how to make this M : A : D BREAKTHROUGH.

We'll live longer and live stronger. We'll live happier and healthier, wealthier and wiser. And so will everyone else.

Unleashing your M : A : D Legacy

For as long as we have the gift of Life, we must nurture every part of it—and that includes ourselves—and others. It includes our creativity, our soul, our spirit, our skills and capabilities—our glorious uniqueness, our magic—and our light.

"Shining" your light "makes the difference" of inspiring others to shine theirs.

This BREAKTHROUGH contains one final secret to unlocking your personal mastery.

The secret to expanding your Legacy exponentially is UNCONDITIONAL M : A : D LOVE.

If, in the journey of creating your Legacy, you focus on deliberate acts of UNCONDITIONAL M : A : D GENEROSITY, the overwhelming sense of joy you'll experience is the ULTIMATE GIFT.

Being "conditional" means that your efforts to leave a Legacy are wasted, as they're driven by ego. Far worse, from ego, any "difference" you make in the short term will ultimately be destructive.

Whatever "difference" you make to someone else—or the World—is simultaneously made within your Self—and, of course, vice versa—WHEN, and only when, it is powered by LOVE.

Authentically, unconditionally M : A : D generosity, Love and connection—this is what our souls cry out for.

Now you have THE KEY—it's time to turn it.

So, the question is . . .

R. U. M : A : D?

Are you...

- **R**andomly

- **U**nconditionally

- "**M**aking : **A** : **D**ifference"?

If so, together we can change ourselves, and the World, one BREAKTHROUGH, one M : A : D deed at a time.

Breakthrough #20

Get a Mentor–
Be a Mentor

Why is it that we so often need a train wreck in our lives to get the energy to fix what's clearly broken?

I think the answer has something to do with us being ready to learn.

There's an old saying that goes:

"When the student is ready, the teacher appears."

As you will have gathered, I have been married three times. I wish I didn't have that score on the board, but that's what it is. I had a couple of serious relationships in between, too, that didn't work out. The inevitable aftermath conversations with friends about the lessons learned yielded the same responses–every time!

Mmmmm . . . what was it Einstein said about needing a new level of thinking to solve a problem? And that old saying about the definition of insanity being repeating the same thing while expecting a different result?

Finding a Mentor

After the demise of my third marriage, which I was very sad about, I decided to do something different.

Finally, the student was ready to learn. I enrolled in a course called "Marriage Mastery." Although it's normally done, indeed was never before not done, as a couple, I decided to embark on the program on my own.

My coaches (a married couple with 30 years of joint therapy experience) agreed to take me on—as an amusing experiment, I think. But I was on a quest to understand what had happened, and what I needed to do differently to be the very best version of myself in my next marriage (assuming I would ever be given the chance!) .

It doesn't really matter what I did with them during that amazing course, although I could write a whole book about it and everything I learned about relationships—and myself. The point is, when I was finally ready to learn, the perfect teacher (for me!) showed up.

What I've learned about the perfect teacher or mentor is that he or she must have no conflict of interest, no hidden agenda, no ax to grind, and no vested interest in the outcome other than the happiness of the "student" or mentee.

What follows is the list of qualities and values that I work hard at delivering to my own mentee clients. You should apply it in the first instance while formulating questions to assess the capabilities of anyone you might be considering as your own mentor.

As you read it, you may like to use TOOL #26 to write down the names of people that you respect, trust and admire who embody each quality. This may well lead you to ask one of them to mentor you on an important BREAKTHROUGH that you are seeking to achieve.

It's a long list, but I trust you will find it useful:

Accountability

I expect and encourage my clients and their corporate sponsors to hold me accountable for helping to make a measurable difference–to provide a yardstick for measuring the effectiveness of the mentoring process. I work from the outset with the client to establish measurable objectives that we review together at regular intervals.

Credibility

Credibility is an essential quality of all meaningful relationships. It is about being believed in, not only for who we are, but also for what we stand for. I have demonstrated competence (and incompetence) in business and in life. This credibility is only ever measured by my clients. If clients do not see me as credible, then I am not credible, no matter what other qualities I have.

Honesty

At all times, I must be 100 percent honest in my feedback to, and interaction with, my clients and adhere to the highest moral and ethical standards. If I cannot help them myself I will say so and source additional support from my extensive network.

Integrity

I make sure that I never have a conflict of interest, hidden agenda, vested interest or ax to grind, either inside or outside the business mentor/client relationship. This is why I only ever take on ten clients at any one time and never have two operating in the same sector of business.

Partnership

Life is a wonderful journey. There are no dress rehearsals. There is no greater privilege than to share a journey of discovery as someone's trusted partner and companion. A mentor acts as a catalyst to success, helping clients find a better way to a better place—to become the best versions of themselves. I help clients plot their journeys on new or different paths. I never abandon clients—yet never let them become dependent on me, either.

Reliability

I strive to be reliable and consistent so that my clients know they can depend on me for quality service at all times. I must deliver on all promises and undertakings made.

Trustworthiness

For me to be effective, I must be trusted. Without trust, scope for exploration is limited. Our starting place is the principle that everything discussed will be kept entirely confidential, forever and without exception. This principle may sometimes extend to maintaining individual client and/or corporate sponsor anonymity.

Goal Orientation

I continually remind my clients that all actions are focused on goals. Regular feedback and measurement processes are set up to generate and sustain momentum, since the more measurable it is, the more manageable it becomes.

Generosity

Karma works. As a mentor I demonstrate leadership through generously giving of my time, contacts and knowledge. Together with my clients I strive to complete each assignment on a personal and professional high.

Commitment

I am committed not only intellectually, but also emotionally to providing the best assistance possible for clients, so that they can progress consistently toward their goals. I have genuine and deeply felt respect for my clients and for my relationship with them.

Communication

Listening and expert information gathering are essential. I need to be able to hear, understand and process information, and use it. I am a sounding board as well as a listening post, who can offer feedback in a way that creates an environment for mutual free expression. I must also recognize the need to be direct with a client without losing rapport or trust, and have the ability to get to the point quickly and effectively, sometimes saying what no one else may be prepared to say.

Empathy

Empathy enables me to gain understanding–vital to generating a strong working relationship. It's not the same as agreement. Indeed there will often be value in the ability to disagree.

Flexibility

I must always be available when needed–and in a position to react swiftly to situations as they arise and to help deliver a bespoke solution.

Objectivity

I aim always to be objective and rational with clients, even when the truth hurts–to be a lighthouse in terms of truth and values, a fixed point shedding light to show the way and highlight dangers.

Patience

Tolerance and the capacity to remain calm and composed in a crisis are essential when clients are grappling with stressful issues. As clients experiment with new ideas, I give them time and personal space in which to reflect and arrive at their own destination, in their own way and in their own time.

Practicality

Theories are interesting, but what distinguishes a successful mentor is the ability to give practical advice when it's needed. The mentor assists in finding expedient and appropriate solutions to challenges, devising with the client bespoke solutions that are specific, measurable and fit for purpose.

Sensitivity

All long-term interpersonal relationships that go below the surface require sensitivity. The starting point is a "passionate disinterest" in a client's nationality, ethnic origin, race, religion, gender, marital status and sexual orientation, coupled with a healthy respect for diversity.

Openness

I value the ability to be vulnerable and open and ruthlessly honest about myself. Disarming honesty creates great trust. In a good mentoring relationship, both mentor and mentee grow and learn. This must be understood at the outset.

Business Understanding

I understand and have a passionate interest in what business is about today. I am both concerned about and have some sense of where it may go in the future. It is part of my own continuous process of learning and development. For these reasons, I host thought-leadership events and founded The Rocket Club. As part of the *kaizen* of my own performance, I keep closely in touch with business publications and attend seminars and other events.

Enjoyment of Life

Life is more than work. Demonstrating our enjoyment of both is essential. Curiosity is one of my own strongest distinguishing features.

Learning

My passion for continued personal growth and learning defines who I am today and who I will become in the future. Learning enables me to be more effective and creative in exploring new ways to make myself useful to my clients.

Emotional Intelligence

Self-awareness, altruism, motivation, empathy, instinct, intuition, and the ability to love and be loved by friends, partners and family members, all go together. People who possess high emotional intelligence are people who truly succeed in work, as well as play, and who build flourishing careers and lasting relationships.

Optimism

What we have experienced in life defines who we are. Challenges are an everyday part of life and should be relished. They are an opportunity to help us be stretched and to stretch others. First-hand experience of setbacks—knowing what is needed to overcome them and to move forward to new and greater successes—are key qualities. Failure isn't falling down, it's staying down. Repeated failure around the same issue can only ever mean an unwillingness or inability to learn from mistakes.

This is by no means an exhaustive list! However, if you find someone who checks off a lot of these boxes, you can assume that they will be a great mentor.

You might also like to think about what other qualities and capabilities you might look for in your ideal mentor.

One of the reasons why people lead unconscious lives, I believe, is that their parents didn't parent (i.e., mentor) them either very well, or at all, and they are still waiting for someone to show up and do so.

My advice? Stop waiting! Find a mentor to support you.

. . . .

I fondly remember being asked to teach a group of complete novices how to ski. If, indeed, I had been the Olympic team skiing champion, as my boss Derek, who gave me the assignment, had erroneously believed was on my résumé, it would have been a breeze!

But, as you may have guessed, I had never been on a pair of skis in my life—or, not at least on snow. The sum total of my skiing experience had been a one-hour lesson during a school trip to a dry ski slope some 15 years earlier.

For the life of me, I can't recall why I thought I could do this, and suspect it had something to do with trying to impress my boss—as a transfer to San Diego was on the cards and I *really* wanted it.

Anyway, I agreed to take on this small group of beginners. I confessed all to a bemused and amused ski instructor at the resort where we were staying in Imst, Austria, and he taught me each day at 6:00 a.m.

for an hour what I, in turn, then had to teach my class after breakfast that same morning.

Who knows how . . . but it worked! And on the final day, we all skied down from the hot chocolate café to base camp like a string of ducks on a pond, much to the joy of my students and the admiration of my boss. San Diego happened less than a year later!

I have always been struck by the saying, **"We teach best the things we most need to learn."**

Without necessarily realizing it, this is often how we Make : A : Difference to the life of someone else.

. . . .

We all have a few basic human needs, one of which is the **need to be heard.** Whether it's coming home from a bad day at work and unloading uninterrupted to a friendly listening post, or sharing with a best friend how excited we are about the potential new love in our lives, or swapping stories with a fellow single parent concerning what to do about the latest episode in the rollercoaster life of our offspring, we all feel so much better after getting it "off our chest" and "out there." As the old British Telecom advertisement said, **"It's good to talk."**

Our next need after being heard is the need to be understood. When someone can really relate to what you are sharing and makes you feel understood, it creates a deep bond between you. (See BREAKTHROUGH #12 and MVE.) To be validated creates a feeling of safety in which even more intimacy can be shared.

Being a Mentor

Your role as a mentor is to be someone experienced and knowledgeable who can listen intelligently and ask probing questions that help the mentee reach a higher level of self-awareness and understanding, so that they can do something differently to get a better result—and become a better version of themselves.

Perhaps you have already been a mentor in the workplace or to kids' sports teams?

I encourage you to review the checklist in TOOL #26 if you feel drawn to step into the role of being a mentor yourself, and to rate yourself against all the items on the list. What qualities do you possess that are your strengths, that would make you a great mentor . . . and what qualities might you need to develop further?

What other capabilities and qualities not listed might you possess that you can offer others as their mentor?

Be generous with your time and your talents in service to someone else. It will make a huge difference to you and you will make as many BREAKTHROUGHs by being a mentor as you will from having one.

· ·

Finding Someone to Mentor

So, how do you go about finding mentees?

You don't! They will show up! They will find you.

When they do, you will feel that their desire to be helped by you mirrors the desire in you to be of service to them.

Mentoring relationships, like all relationships, can last for a reason, a season or a lifetime. The only way to become a great mentor is to be a good one. And becoming a good mentor requires practice. Anywhere is a great place to start.

The **benefits to your mentees** are that you will help them become the best versions of themselves.

The **benefits to you** are that in doing so, you will become the best version of yourself.

It is a privilege to be a mentor.

Making : A : Difference to others is what life is all about.

What we do for ourselves alone dies with us. What we do for others and the world remains and is immortal.

Where to from here ... ?

CONNECT ... with the BREAKTHROUGH Community

Now that you've read BREAKTHROUGH, you are invited to become a member of David C. M. Carter's BREAKTHROUGH community.

Visit **www.davidcmcarter.com** to subscribe to the BREAKTHROUGH blog and newsletter. Each month, various BREAKTHROUGH ideas in this book are expanded upon, explored and further explained to assist you in achieving your own personal BREAKTHROUGH.

You can also subscribe to David C. M. Carter's YouTube channel for the latest video content, including speeches, TV appearances and tutorials to help individuals become the best versions of themselves.

Subscribe at:

www.youtube.com/davidcmcarter

CONNECT WITH . . . The Mentor

Connect directly with The Mentor on LinkedIn–just search for David C. M. Carter–or follow him on Facebook and Twitter for updates about speaking appearances, blog posts and new videos.

Facebook: **www.facebook.com/davidcmcarter**

Twitter: **@davidcmcarter**

JOIN US . . . at
"The BREAKTHROUGH M : A : D RETREAT"

As well as mentoring his 10 select international clients on a 1:1 basis, David and his team of specialists also facilitate the experiential BREAKTHROUGH M : A : D RETREAT.

Retreats are held in spectacular "once-in-a-lifetime" locations and tailored for small groups of 10+ individuals. Retreats can also be arranged for teams, business partners and couples by request.

Register your interest in attending a RETREAT by e-mailing:
breakthrough@davidcmcarter.com

ENGAGE . . . David as a Speaker

David is a much sought-after speaker on the international circuit. He uses engaging stories to convey his messages about mentoring, being the best version of yourself and Making : A : Difference—as well as a host of other subjects encompassing everything from Leadership to Life!

Contact David
breakthrough@davidcmcarter.com

Breakthrough Retreat Workbook

Introduction

Now that you have read through the 20 BREAKTHROUGHs, you are ready to enter **THE ZONE**.

The simple TOOLs that follow cover all the BREAKTHROUGHs you've read about.

None of them cost money, and they don't take a great deal of time to complete.

The BREAKTHROUGH RETREAT WORKBOOK TOOLs can be approached in a number of ways:

1. You can work through them on your own (least recommended)

2. You can offer to work through them with someone else as a mentor—or as a mentee (recommended) or . . .

3. You can work with a learning partner and mentor each other as you do it together (most highly recommended).

Whichever approach you choose, you will be laying the foundation stones for a life of personal mastery.

The exercises are designed to explore the following six areas in your life:

1. Where am I at right now in my life and how do I define success moving forward from here?

2. What are my values?

3. What are my strengths, gifts and talents?

4. How do I manage my time?

5. How balanced are the Spokes in my Wheel of Life?

6. Am I in the ZONE?

Please make sure you set aside some quality time to do the exercises and that you do them in a place where you'll feel relaxed and connected to your authentic Self.

Even if you've already tackled a few of these TOOLs and techniques as you were reading through BREAKTHROUGH, it's always valuable to revisit them. In fact, I highly recommend that you do so regularly—and do them in the various ways I've suggested; i.e., with a mentor or learning partner and also mentoring someone else.

The BREAKTHROUGH RETREAT WORKBOOK is also available as a FREE DOWNLOAD from my website at **www.davidcmcarter.com**.

Regardless of whether you have a hard copy or digital version of BREAKTHROUGH, you have no excuse to not do the exercises—other than you have not yet chosen to be the best version of yourself!

Although not quite as intimate or fun as working 1:1 with you myself, I trust that this program will not only enable you to make all the BREAKTHROUGHs you choose, but that you will also thoroughly enjoy doing it . . . and sharing the experience with others.

So, what you waiting for? Dive in!

David C. M. Carter

Tool #1

My Top Priorities

What are the top three priorities in your life right now?

It may be to "get a new job," "fix my marriage," "fend off an unwanted hostile takeover," "find a cure for cancer," "lose weight," "save some money" or "relax more." There are no right or wrong answers here.

We'll be repeating this exercise again at the end to see whether any priorities have changed for you. Feel free to return to this exercise and review and change this list as you work through the rest of the TOOLs. Here goes . . .

The top three priorities in my life at the moment are . . .

1.

2.

3.

Tool #2

Where Am I Now?

Identify and list all of the various roles in your life; e.g., father/mother, son/daughter, husband/wife/partner, CEO, friend, community member, Self, etc. What are the goals linked to each role?

My most important roles and goals are . . .

Role	Goal	% Satisfied

Next, please score your overall level of satisfaction with your own performance in each role (not the way others score you, but the way you score yourself).

Tool #3

Establishing Your Purpose in Life

If you could write the inscription on your own tombstone, what would you like it to say? For what would you best like to be remembered?

Tool #4

Beyond Fear of Failing

If you *knew* that it was not possible to fail, that you could only fall over and pick yourself back up again, what would you do?

If I knew I could not fail, I would . . .

_____

_____

_____

_____

_____

_____

_____

_____

_____

_____

Tool #5

My Successful Decade

Imagine that in ten years you are looking back over your life. Describe what you will have done that will mean you consider your life to have been successful.

I will consider my life to have been successful if . . .

_____

_____

_____

_____

_____

_____

_____

_____

_____

Tool #6

My Three "Critical Action" Items for Success

The next ten years are made up of ten one-year plans.

Identify the critical things to "action" that, if you focus on them for the next 12 months, will give you the best chance of achieving success.

The three mission-critical things that I can do in the next year to give myself the greatest chance of success are . . .

1.

_____

_____

_____

2.

_____

_____

_____

3.

_____

_____

_____

Tool #7

My Values, Beliefs and Behaviors

Do you know what motivates your behavior? It's time to explore the link between your values, beliefs and behaviors, and the emotional ties that you have to certain values.

Read through the list of Positive Values and select the Top 10 that are very important for you to have in your life. If there are words that you feel you would like to include, add them to the list.

e.g.

Accountability	Creativity	Generosity	Persistence
Achievement	Dedication	Growth	Personal fulfillment
Adventure	Dependability	Happiness	Personal growth
Ambition	Determination	Health	Power

Once you have identified your Top 10, write them alphabetically on the Ranking Positive Values table in both the horizontal row and the vertical column.

Using the vertical column as your first point of reference, compare the first value in the vertical column with the first value in the horizontal row. They are the same, therefore of equal importance to you, so the square is shaded.

Then compare the first vertical value with the second horizontal value and decide if the vertical value is MORE important for you to have in your life.

	1	2	3
Positive Values **Compare against**	Adventure	Generosity	Personal growth
1 Adventure	■	✓	✓
2 Generosity	✗	■	✓
3 Personal growth	✗	✗	■

If it is MORE important, give it a ✔.

If it is LESS important, insert an ✗.

Then compare the first vertical value with the third horizontal value and decide if the vertical value is MORE important. Once again . . .

If it is MORE important, give it a ✔.

If it is LESS important, insert an ✗.

Continue in this way until you have a ✔ or an ✗ in all boxes.

When you have completed the entire grid, total up the checks in each row.

In theory, one column will have nine checks in it, one will have eight checks, and so on down to zero checks.

If it doesn't work out like this, it's because one time you thought that "adventure" was more important than "personal growth," but when presented with the choice the other way around, you thought that "personal growth" was more important than "adventure."

When you have determined your Positive Values ranking from one to ten, list your top three in the final table. Then repeat this exercise to identify your Negative Values.

Identification of Positive Values

Accountability	Creativity	Generosity	Persistence
Achievement	Dedication	Growth	Personal fulfillment
Adventure	Dependability	Happiness	Personal growth
Ambition	Determination	Health	Power
Attraction	Discipline	Honesty	Prosperity
Balance (home/work)	Ecstasy	Humility	Quality
Beauty	Efficiency	Humor/fun	Respect
Challenge	Enthusiasm	Independence	Responsibility
Choice	Environmental awareness	Initiative	Risk taking
Clarity	Ethics	Integrity	Safety
Cooperation	Excellence	Intuition	Security
Commitment	Excitement	Job security	Self-confidence
Communication	Fairness	Joy	Self-discipline
Community involvement	Family	Listening	Spiritual unity
Compassion	Financial stability	Logic	Strength
Competence	Flexibility	Love	Success
Competition	Forgiveness	Loyalty	Support
Confidence	Freedom	Making a difference	Trustworthiness
Conflict resolution	Friendship	Mission focus	Vision
Continuous learning	Fun	Openness	Wisdom
Courage	Future generations	Perseverance	???

Ranking Positive Values

	1	2	3	4	5	6	7	8	9	10	Total
Positive Values Compare Against											
1											
2											
3											
4											
5											
6											
7											
8											
9											
10											

Identification of Negative Values

Rejection	Anger	Humiliation	Worry
Depression	Regret	Misery	Sorrow
Frustration	Embarrassment	Despair	Poverty
Failure	Discouragement	Cynicism	Rigidity
Self-doubt	Hostility	Pessimism	Sadness
Bitterness	Futility	Gloom	Resignation
Anxiety	Criticism	Despondency	Judgment
Loneliness	Greed	Jealousy	Condemnation
Guilt	Lethargy	Suspicion	Disinterest
Disappointment	Ostracism	Withdrawal	Fear of (specify)

After completing the stack ranking in the same way you did earlier for the Positive Values, then list the Top 3 in the next table.

This time indicate with a ✔ the value that is WORSE for you. So, if "rejection" is more abhorrent to you than "jealousy," give it a ✔. If it's worse than all the other Negative Values on your list of ten, it will have nine checks in the right column.

Ranking Negative Values

		1	2	3	4	5	6	7	8	9	10	Total
Negative Values Compare Against												
1												
2												
3												
4												
5												
6												
7												
8												
9												
10												

Top 3 Positive vs. Top 3 Negative Values

Write down your **Top 3 Positive Values** and **Top 3 Negative Values**.

What beliefs do you have behind each value?

What behaviors do you exhibit that are related to each value and related belief?

Values	Beliefs	Behaviors
#1 Positive		
#1 Negative		
#2 Positive		
#2 Negative		
#3 Positive		
#3 Negative		

Tool #8

My Superstrengths

People sometimes find it hard to describe their strengths. Strangely, however, they find it easier to describe their "Superstrengths." Why? Perhaps it's because they find it easier to highlight the few things that they do brilliantly?

What are your Top 3 Superstrengths?

My Superstrengths are . . .

I can . . .

_____

_____

_____

I can . . .

_____

_____

_____

I can . . .

_____

_____

_____

Tool #9

Balls in Bowls

Visual, hands-on exercise brings greater insights than a solely verbal approach.

Equipment:

8   Cereal bowls

12   Ping-Pong balls

16+   Sticky notes (approx. 4″ squares) to label bowls

Method: Lay out the eight bowls and label each of the bowls as an area of your current life (e.g., work, family, hobbies, spiritual, etc.). You do not have to label all of the bowls. Consider whether the labeling truly reflects the scope of your life.

Next, place all twelve balls in the appropriate bowls to reflect how you use your time and energy today. Balls are not divisible and all must be used.

Make a note of the current distribution of the balls. How satisfied are you with the current situation?

Based on your answer, begin the process of identifying any desirable changes in these areas of your life.

Next, "reshape" your life, using the balls, bowls and labels, to a new model that reflects your dreams.

Consider the implications emerging from this new paradigm.

Tool #10

My Daily Disciplines

The daily disciplines I must do to reach my highest purpose are . . .

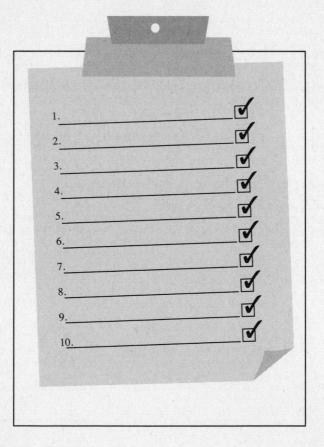

1.
2.
3.
4.
5.
6.
7.
8.
9.
10.

Tool #11

More : Start : Continue : Stop

Think back over the last year.

What activities gave you energy and made you feel great?

What did you want to do and perhaps didn't, that might have made you feel great?

I would like to do MORE of . . .

_____

_____

I'm not yet involved in or doing, but would like to START doing . . .

_____

_____

I would like to CONTINUE doing . . .

_____

_____

I receive little enjoyment from, and/or would like to eliminate or STOP doing . . .

_____

_____

Tool #12

Balancing My
Wheel of Life

If the bull's-eye in the middle represents zero percent, the middle ring 50 percent, and the outer ring 100 percent, please mark an ✗ in each of the six areas to rate your level of satisfaction with your performance in this area of your life.

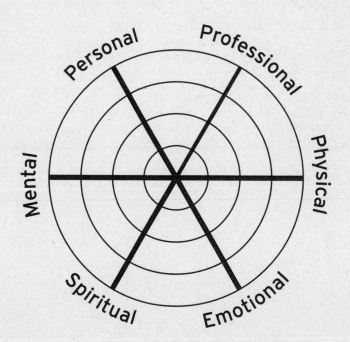

Tool #13

The Six Spokes

For it to really "hum," your Wheel of Life requires well-balanced Spokes, so let's take a closer look at each of them in turn.

First, in the central circle, write the various roles you play in your life; e.g., father/mother, son/daughter, husband/wife/partner, CEO, leader, friend, community member, etc.

Think about the commitments and values that you have within each of these roles and how they impact each of the six Spokes.

In each of the six circles extending from the Spokes, identify and write down the key items for each of these six areas of your life that will help you become the best version of yourself.

Next, use the relevant table on the following pages to zero in on each of those six circles (i.e., Professional, Personal, Mental, Physical, Spiritual and Emotional). List the NEED associated with that key item (sometimes the item can be the need!)—and any ACTIONS required.

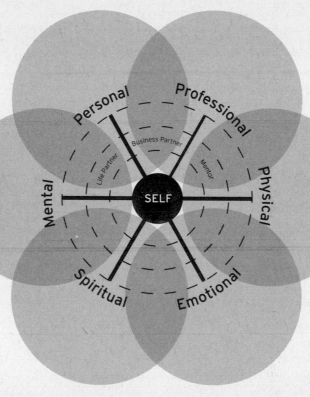

PROFESSIONAL

NEEDS	ACTIONS

PERSONAL

NEEDS	ACTIONS

MENTAL

NEEDS	ACTIONS

PHYSICAL

NEEDS	ACTIONS

SPIRITUAL

NEEDS	ACTIONS

EMOTIONAL

NEEDS	ACTIONS

MY BUCKET LIST

And finally, what goes on your Bucket List . . . what things are an absolute MUST for you to feel complete in your life?

1
2
3
4
5
6
7

Tool #14

In "The Zone"

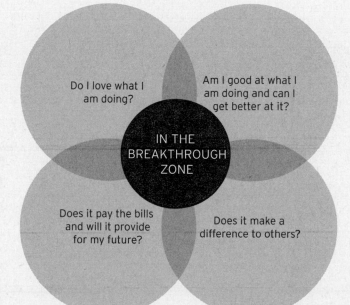

Do I love what I am doing?

Am I good at what I am doing and can I get better at it?

IN THE BREAKTHROUGH ZONE

Does it pay the bills and will it provide for my future?

Does it make a difference to others?

What is required for you to do your most extraordinary work? One way is to identify the following situations and activities that put you in The Zone.

Where, and doing what, do you feel totally in flow, at ease and able to excel?

How can you capitalize on these situations and activities?

The situation(s) where I feel in The Zone, where I feel in flow, at ease and able to excel, is/are . . .

_____

_____

_____

_____

_____

The specific steps and/or ways that I support myself to stay in The Zone and excel are . . .

_____

_____

_____

_____

_____

The steps I can take to spend even more time in The Zone and excel in the future are . . .

_____

_____

_____

_____

_____

Tool #15

My Energy Givers and Energy Takers

The things that GIVE me energy are . . .

_____

_____

_____

_____

_____

The things that TAKE, or deplete, my energy are . . .

_____

_____

_____

_____

_____

Tool #16

My Guaranteed Income

If you had a guaranteed income for the rest of your life, what would you do? Initially you might travel the world, buy all the things on your "wish list," and lavish friends and family with gifts. But then what? Go deeper. What really DRIVES you? What would give you a sense of fulfillment?

If I had a guaranteed income for the rest of my life, I would . . .

_____

_____

_____

_____

_____

_____

_____

_____

Tool #17

Finding Fulfillment

What activities do you find fulfilling? Try to be as specific as possible. If you wish, you can include things from both your personal and professional life.

The things I find fulfilling are . . .

_____

_____

_____

_____

What steps can you take to do more of these things?

The steps I can take to do more of these fulfilling things are . . .

_____

_____

_____

_____

Tool #18

Wisdom Council

The five people I will invite to form/join my Wisdom Council are . . .

1.

_____

2.

_____

3.

_____

4.

_____

5.

_____

Tool #19

Road-Mapping
My Future

1. List the possible roads or directions you can take in a particular life scenario, or "Spoke" in your Wheel of Life; e.g., in your Professional Spoke:

a) Stay in my present work (or relationship / home / country, etc.)

b) Move to another job inside the same organization

c) Move to a competitor

d) Do something completely different

2. Describe the pluses and minuses of each option.

3. Rate how attractive each option is to you on a scale of zero to ten.

With this overview of the different roads you can take, what is your preferred road?

What are the best parts of the other roads?

Is there a new road that includes the best parts of each road?

A	B	C
To:	To:	To:
Pluses	Pluses	Pluses
Minuses	Minuses	Minuses
Attractiveness Rating	Attractiveness Rating	Attractiveness Rating
... /10	... /10	... /10

Tool #20

The Stream

This exercise uses "stream of consciousness" writing to list words that describe you and all your talents, skills and gifts—everything that makes you unique. (See BREAKTHROUGH #16 for an example.)

Simply follow the formula below, listing any words that come to mind—and keep going!!! You can also ask others to contribute (friends, your boss, your partner, your parents, your kids). Just keep asking yourself:

What are the things I know about myself that no one else ever sees?

_____ is
[Your Name]

_____

_____

_____

_____

_____

_____

_____

_____

Tool #21

My Goals Posters

You will need:

- two big pieces of card stock (poster size is ideal)
- two identical sets of 30-40 magazines
- Glue
- Scissors
- Crayons

Cut out images from one of the sets of magazines that visually reflect exactly how you would like your life to look and be at a particular date or age in 2-10 years' time, and stick them on the board (e.g., car, home, golf, Caribbean, sunshine, snow, new kitchen, penthouse in New York, kids, dog, happy, healthy, etc.).

Cut out images from the second set of magazines that visually reflect how you feel you live in your environment today, and stick them on the board (e.g., computer screen, calculator, mortgage payments, telephones, pizza, commuting on the subway, etc.).

This is a very powerful tool for goal setting or life visioning. By designing your "Picture of Perfection," you will understand what you really want and why. It will almost certainly tie in to your values and dream lists, and therefore help you to devise a strategy to achieve success.

After you have completed this, set the two boards up side by side so you can see the journey from one board to the other. Feel what you like and love about what is on the left-hand side TODAY board. And also notice what you are not happy about and want to move away from.

Then study the FUTURE board very closely. Imagine you are living in that future state. How will you FEEL to be doing those activities, having those things, achieving those successes? Feel it. Believe it. Hold on to the dream. Make it happen!

Take your time and really think through all of the components of your dream life. Then sit back and watch it unfold as you focus on making it happen.

(See BREAKTHROUGH #3.)

Tool #22

100 Things I Am Grateful For

Make a list of 100 things in your life that you are grateful for. Yes, 100!

When you've finished, if you tell me you don't feel happier than when you started writing the list, I won't believe you!

(See BREAKTHROUGH #6.)

Tool #23

100 Things That Make Me Happy

Make a list of 100 things in your life that make you happy. Yes, 100!

This is a great way of focusing on what you choose for your life, so be mindful to list things you choose to move toward, rather than away from! And just like doing your Gratitude List (TOOL #22), it's guaranteed to boost your happiness levels!

(See BREAKTHROUGH #6.)

Tool #24

Managing My Time

You'll need four different-colored highlighter pens—red, orange, yellow and green. Then print out the PAST six months and the FUTURE six months from your diary. Starting with the PAST six months, mark up the pages with each highlighter in turn, as indicated:

RED: Highlight the things in your diary that absolutely should have been deleted and that were a complete waste of your time.

ORANGE: Highlight the things that someone else in your organization could or should have done and that you should have delegated.

Now, calculate the percentage of time wasted on things that could or should have been deleted (RED) or delegated (ORANGE).

YELLOW: Highlight times where you were learning, growing, developing, and preparing yourself for the next stage.

GREEN: Highlight the times when you were being the very best version of yourself, when you were flying high, playing to your strengths, absolutely in The Zone and where you are the only person in the organization who could have been doing what you were doing.

Now repeat the exact same exercise in your diary with the FUTURE six months.

It's time to make some courageous decisions about what needs to change moving forward! (See BREAKTHROUGH #4.)

Tool #25

"3D" Prioritizing—Do, Delegate, Delete

If I were to use the 3D Approach to prioritizing my tasks, I would . . .

DO—*the things I want to and need to do/drive are . . .*

_____

_____

DELEGATE—*the following things that I want and need to give to someone else to do . . .*

_____

_____

DELETE—*the following things that I want and need to "ditch" and divest myself of . . .*

_____

_____

Tool #26

Mentor and Mentee

1. Finding a Mentor: Are you considering finding a mentor? To assess whether the mentor has capabilities that are a good fit for your needs, you might like to apply the following list of qualities and values. These are the ones that I work hard at delivering to my own mentee clients. It's quite a long list, but I trust you will find it useful.

As you read it, write down the names of people that you respect, trust and admire who embody each quality. This may well lead you to ask one of them to mentor you on an important BREAKTHROUGH that you are seeking to achieve.

It is by no means an exhaustive list—you may want to add some additional qualities and capabilities that you are looking for in your ideal mentor. However, if you find someone who checks off a lot of these boxes, you can probably assume that he or she will be a great mentor.

2. Being a Mentor: Do you feel drawn to step into the role of being a mentor yourself?

If so, rate yourself against all the items on the list, identifying which qualities and strengths you possess that would make you a great mentor—and which qualities you might need to develop further?

What additional capabilities do you possess that you can include in this list and that you can offer others as a mentor?

Qualities of a Great Mentor

Qualities	Candidate	Me
Accountability		
Credibility		
Honesty		
Integrity		
Partnership		
Reliability		
Trustworthiness		
Goal orientation		
Generosity		
Commitment		
Communication		
Empathy		
Flexibility		
Objectivity		
Patience		
Practicality		
Sensitivity		
Openness		
Business understanding		
Enjoyment of life		
Learning		
Emotional intelligence		
Optimism		

Tool #27

Heart of the Matter

The Top 10 "must have" qualities for me to have in relationships are . . .

1. _____
2. _____
3. _____
4. _____
5. _____
6. _____
7. _____
8. _____
9. _____
10. _____

Tool #28

My Move Mountains Mental Menu

For this exercise, you'll need to mentally prepare yourself the night before to begin from the moment you wake up the next morning.

I promise you, it's much harder than you think. You won't naturally think "always positive" thoughts about people or situations. Having to restrain your tongue from reacting to your thoughts as quickly as it normally does requires practice. But persevere. I guarantee that you will feel different—and the people you interact with will respond positively.

DAY 1: Commit to yourself from the moment you wake up that every single word that comes out of your mouth for the whole day will be positive, affirming and empowering.

Record some of the new words and phrases that you adopt and would like to continue to use . . .

_____

_____

_____

DAY 2: Continue with your commitment from yesterday—with a new addition. Today, extend yourself by deliberately seeking out new positive words and phrases. Put real effort into expanding your range of positive vocabulary and notice the impact this has on the people you interact with.

Record more of your new words and phrases that you would like to continue to use...

_____

_____

_____

_____

DAY 3: Today, after each positive interaction or episode, add in an acknowledgment of your gratitude for the situation, the person, your circumstances—or whatever it is you are pleased and positive about.

*For example, "AND, in relation to this positive encounter, I feel **grateful** for..."*

_____

_____

_____

_____

Tool #29

My Top Priorities Review

Congratulations on completing the BREAKTHROUGH RETREAT WORKBOOK!

This may seem like "the end"—but if you've achieved even just one of the BREAKTHROUGHs in this book, it's actually a new beginning!

Please review your Top 3 priorities from TOOL #1 and notice whether any have changed?

My Top 3 priorities moving forward are now . . .

1.
2.
3.

Notes

Notes

Notes

Notes

Notes

Notes

Notes

Notes

Notes

Notes

Notes

Notes

Notes

David C. M. Carter is widely regarded as one of the world's leading mentors. He has an exclusive list of just ten clients at any one time, ranging from CEOs of major companies, to entrepreneurs, celebrities and philanthropists.

During his twenties, David spent ten years in banking and private equity (in the US, UK, Europe, Middle and Far East), followed by another decade in his thirties as an entrepreneur in the UK leisure sector, including two start-ups, one of which was sold, and the second launched on the Alternative Investment Market.

After 20 years of apprenticeship in business and life, David spent the next 14 years building and leading, as Founder, CEO and Chairman, Merryck & Co., which eventually became the world's leading CEO Business Mentoring Company. In 2010, he exited—and subsequently reinvented and relaunched himself as THE MENTOR—through using most of the BREAKTHROUGH techniques that he now shares with you in this, his first book.

He has enjoyed the highest of personal and business successes, as well as survived a few failures and near disasters, each time making a comeback as a "better version of himself." He enjoys recounting the tales of his adventures and sharing the lessons he's learned and the wisdom he's gained.

David is the proud father of two children whom he has parented, mostly single-handedly, since 1995. A hopeful romantic, he is based in London and enjoys golf, learning to play blues harmonica, home-cooked food, movies, live music, Mediterranean sunshine and regular road trips in his beloved convertible.